Rebels without a Cause?

AGGLETON   P

Rebels without a cause?
: middle class youth
and the transition
from school to work

London, New York, and Philadelphia.

Issues in Education and Training Series: 8

Rebels without a Cause?

Middle Class Youth and the Transition from School to Work

Peter Aggleton

 The Falmer Press

(A member of the Taylor & Francis Group)
London New York and Philadelphia

UK The Falmer Press, Falmer House, Barcombe, Lewes, East Sussex, BN8 5DL

USA The Falmer Press, Taylor & Francis Inc., 242 Cherry Street, Philadelphia, PA 19106-1906

First published 1987

Library of Congress Cataloguing in Publication Data is available on request

ISBN 1-85000-224-X
ISBN 1-85000-225-8 (pbk.)

Jacket design by Caroline Archer

Typeset in 11/13 Bembo by
Imago Publishing Ltd, Thame, Oxon

Printed in Great Britain by Taylor & Francis (Printers) Ltd, Basingstoke

Contents

Preface

Academic underachievement has long been of interest to teachers and educationalists, as have been the forms of 'resistance' employed by disaffected young people in schools and colleges. This book presents findings from a three-year ethnographic study of a group of 'underachieving' students in an English college of further education. It identifies patterns of cultural affirmation and 'resistance' amongst young people from new middle class backgrounds, and examines the relationship between these and the students' home and out-of-college lives. The study also examines the consequences of new middle class youth cultural styles for the reproduction of class and gender relations, and raises questions about the radical significance, or otherwise, of middle class 'resistance' to schooling.

I am grateful to the Social Science Research Council (subsequently renamed the Economic and Social Research Council) for its financial support in carrying out this study and to the following individuals for their helpful comments on all or parts of the text: Basil Bernstein, John Fitz, Leslie Rothaus, Laurie Taylor, Marilyn Toft, Geoff Whitty and Philip Wexler.

Marlene Bertrand, Bob Giddings, Barbara Lee, Andy Patrick, Clive Symons and Julia Vernon-Smith provided me with unfailing personal support throughout the study. Amongst my colleagues at Bristol Polytechnic, I would like to thank Len Barton, Hilary Homans and Geoff Whitty for encouraging me during the production of the final text. I owe a special debt to Helen Thomas whose wordprocessing of key sections in the manuscript was of the highest order. But above all, I must thank the staff and students of Spatown College for their support and cooperation throughout the three years in which the study was carried out.

Chapter 1

Origins

Introduction

There are likely to be many sources of impetus behind any piece of social or educational research. Some of these take their origin from the *topical* concerns of researchers themselves. Other more *generic* interests have their origin in debates and incoherences within existing bodies of theory. It is the coming together of these twin sources of impetus that establishes a particular research trajectory and the issues which it is likely to address.

In this book I will describe some of the findings which emerged from a three-year study of a group of young people from new middle class backgrounds attending a college of further education in Southern England for the General Certificate of Education (GCE) Advanced ('A') level study. In particular, attention will be focussed on factors associated with the low level of educational attainment which characterized this group of students and on developing explanations which identify the broader social consequences of this apparent educational 'underachievement'.

Topical Concerns

Between 1977 and 1980 I worked as a social science teacher at a college of further education in a small city in Southern England, which I will call Spatown. Spatown is a city which possesses relatively little traditional industry, and many of its residents are employed in administrative, educational and other professional occupations. Being also a major tourist centre with historic associations with the arts, Spatown has attracted as residents many members of the new middle class and, in particular, that fraction of the class which Bernstein (1977) has termed *agents of symbolic control*: those concerned with the dissemination of implicit forms of social control. Hence, living in Spatown were many artists, writers, musicians, performing artists, as well as teachers in further and higher education and others working in the field of personal development and growth.

Three years teaching GCE social science subjects at Spatown College and talking informally with those following these courses helped me begin to understand why a college of further education, rather than the sixth-form of a school, might be preferred by some young people for post-16 academic study. Concurrently, my leisure-time involvement in community arts projects in the same city by chance enabled me to meet many of the parents of those whom I taught. In consequence, it proved possible to gain some insight into parental perceptions of their daughters' and sons' transition from school to college of further education. Additionally, three years spent justifying the dyed and spiked hair of these same students, their forthright manner of response to tutors when challenged about non-attendance at class or the failure to hand in previously set written work, and their occasional drunkenness in class, further compounded my desire to investigate the factors responsible for these particular modes of educational and cultural practice.

By the time these interests had developed to the point at which I felt it useful to carry out a serious academic study of those attending the college, a number of issues had been more clearly identified. Five sets of concerns in particular helped shape my original research agenda.

First, in 1980, post-16 education in Spatown was available either in one of five single sex schools with sixth-forms or at Spatown College. Each year, a number of students chose the latter for GCE Advanced level study rather than one of the nearby schools. Underlying such choices were a number of factors. These included students' own expectations that life at college would be freer than it had been at school, as well as the availability at the college of GCE subjects such as theatre studies, communication and media studies and history of art — none of which were offered as part of local sixth-form provision. Additionally, parental encouragement to make the transition seemed to be an important factor contributing to the move in a number of cases. However, my work within the college suggested that factors of a rather different order might also contribute to decisions such as these. Within a short of time of working there, for example, it became apparent that the students who made this move were remarkably homogeneous in terms of their social background. Most came from homes in which one or both parents were teachers or those working in the theatre, media or creative arts. I was initially intrigued about why this should be the case, and what specifically might be the less readily identifiable processes contributing to the transition.

Second, at the time when I began fieldwork, Spatown College was somewhat distinctive in that within it there were clear social and administrative divisions between the Department of Science, in which GCE science and mathematics subjects were taught, and the Department of General Studies, in which the humanities and social sciences could be studied. In the late 1970s the former of these two departments recruited the majority of its students from the Middle East and Malaysia. The Department of General Studies, in contrast, gained most of its students from the Spatown community itself. In consequence, most of the local students who made the transition from school to college for post-16 GCE study did so in order to study subjects such as English literature, history of art, fine art, communication and theatre studies as well as, to a lesser extent, psychology and sociology.

Third, in the opinion of members of the teaching staff working in the college's Department of General Studies at that time, many students in the Department performed less well in the public examinations that took place at the end of their GCE courses than might reasonably have been expected. In staff meetings and informal discussions prior to, and during, the fieldwork, staff were frequently heard to pass comment on instances of 'underachievement' amongst full-time GCE Advanced level students. In support of such arguments, reference would often be made to discrepancies between an individual student's GCE Ordinary level and Advanced level grades.

Fourth, teaching staff in this same Department frequently explained these perceived patterns of 'underachievement' in terms of the extent to which students' social lives outside of College interferred with their academic study. Both in staff meetings and informally, they expressed the view that students spent too much time in public houses and clubs, at parties and in part-time jobs, for them to be able to get on with the 'hard work' necessary for success in GCE examinations. Informal observations on my own part confirmed the face validity of these interpretations. In their first year at college, students could be found most evenings of the week in one of a limited number of local public houses or clubs. By their second year, most had found part-time work behind the bars in such settings or alternatively in a variety of fast food restaurants and takeaways in the city.

Finally, my own preliminary observations in sub-cultural contexts such as these, had begun to raise a number of questions concerning why certain public houses and clubs came to be chosen for social activity outside of College while others were less popular. In particular, I became intrigued by why it was that preferred settings were those popular with older students from the local University and Polytechnic. Furthermore, it seemed interesting to explore why commercial discotheques well-liked by those of a similar age to college students, were so obviously avoided. Additionally, I was interested in finding out why talk of overseas films and twentieth-century literature, of radical politics and nuclear disarmament, occupied so much of students' time. These and many other questions relating to the educational and social consequences of a relatively under-researched set of middle class educational and social practices formed a powerful impetus behind the research described in this book.

Generic Concerns

Students, Schools and Schooling

Since the early 1960s, a central focus within educational research has been students' experience of schools and schooling. Early small-scale interpretative studies of school experience, such as those carried out by Werthman (1963), Hargreaves (1967) and Lacey (1970), helped establish a tradition of enquiry in which primacy came to be given to the processes of interaction within schools through which sub-cultural differentiation takes place. Many of these investigations sought to combine the interpretative sensitivity of ethnographic research methods with insights derived more generally from interactionist sociology. As a result, they aimed to explore the *meaningfulness* of different types of student response to schooling, the processes of *negotiation* by which social identities came to be constructed and the mechanisms by which *school deviance* arises. In recent years, interactionist and social phenomenological studies by Woods (1979), Ball (1981), Turner (1983) and Pollard (1985) have extended these earlier analyses of school experience by identifying, amongst other things, typologies detailing the wide range of responses students can give to schooling.

The 1970s also saw an increase in sociological interest in the origins and effects of youth sub-cultural responses outside of schools. The critical readings of Ted, Mod and Skinhead style offered by researchers at the Centre for Contemporary Cultural Studies in Birmingham (Jefferson, 1975; Hebdige, 1975; Clarke, 1975) quickly called into question the adequacy of previous structural-functionalist (see for example Eisenstadt, 1956; Coleman, 1961) and interactionist (see, for example, Wieder and Zimmerman, 1974; Simmon and Trout, 1967) explanations of youth sub-cultures. Neither of these approaches, it was argued, could adequately account for the historical specificity of contemporary youth sub-cultural styles. Nor could they account for the class-based nature of young people's responses to changing economic and social conditions. The more materialist analyses of youth that resulted from work at the Centre for Contemporary Cultural Studies (CCCS) sought subsequently to remedy both of these problems by combining an interpretative sensitivity to the nature of lived cultural experience with a more thoroughgoing analysis of the historical and material conditions which give rise to specific sub-cultural responses.

Operating with many of the methodological commitments advocated by those seeking concurrently to develop the 'new criminology' (Taylor, Walton and Young, 1973 and 1975), CCCS researchers enquired into the relationship between youth sub-cultures and broader economic and social determinants. For a while, identifying homologies, resonances and tensions between sub-cultural style and its historical and material determinants became a major preoccupation amongst researchers of this persuasion. Youth sub-cultures were said to 'magically resolve' the material contradictions facing young people (Cohen, 1972), being both logical and practical responses to life in modern class-based societies. According to such analyses, British youth cultural styles in the post-war period were best interpreted as symbolic forms of resistance to the dominant social order, being symptoms of wider and submerged class dissent. Analyzing them, therefore, required both a detailed examination of the class locations occupied by their members and of the particular material contradictions associated with these.

Culture, Ideology and Social Reproduction

Underpinning much of the work at CCCS were a number of inter-related concerns. The first of these was a response to earlier calls for research to illuminate more fully the distinctive social relationships that characterize specifically working class culture (Williams, 1958; Thompson, 1963). In consequence, it is perhaps not surprising that the youth sub-cultures which came largely to be focussed on in the work of researchers associated with CCCS were those which were largely working class in origin.

A second concern related more closely to the wish to explore more fully the relationships between cultural forms and their structural determinants. In looking back over research conducted at this time, Johnson (1979) has argued that much of it was motivated by the desire to produce,

> ... a proper assessment of the character of such moments (of cultural practice) by placing them within a wider analysis of economic and social structures. This required conceptual tools for a properly historicized account of capitalism's continuing economic transformations and of the positions of groups of men and women in relation to it and to each other ...

The various projects carried out at CCCS throughout this period (Hall and Jefferson, 1975; CCCS, 1977; Women's Studies Group, 1978), of which research into youth sub-cultures formed only one strand, were given considerable impetus by insights from concurrently developing neo-Marxist analyses of ideology and the social formation. In seeking to extend Marx's (1932) original claim that 'It is not the consciousness of men that determines their being, but, on the contrary, their social being that determines their consciousness', writers such as Althusser (1969 and 1971) had, by the mid-1970s, begun to develop more sophisticated analyses of the social formation as a set of interrelated levels, sites and practices. Steering a course between the dangers of overly humanistic and overly economistic modes of explanation, however, proved far from easy. In consequence, whilst Althusser (1976) himself took pains to argue that the relationship between the economy, legal, political and ideological relations and individual subjectivity is far from direct, his work came, nevertheless, to be accused by Johnson (1979) and others of an inherent functionalism. In his analysis of the processes by which social relations within capitalism come to be reproduced, for example, Johnson claims that Althusser,

> ... represents reproduction, which, in Marx, is necessarily a contradictory and antagonistic process, as a functional necessity of a system. ... What is correctly understood as a condition or a contingency becomes, in the course of the argument, a continuously achieved outcome. Dominant ideology, organized especially through apparatuses such as schools, works with all the certainty normally ascribed to natural or biological processes. We are returned to a very familiar model of one-

dimensional control in which all sense of struggle or contradiction is lost . . .

In order to guard against this 'creeping functionalism', researchers at CCCS and elsewhere sought to forge an alliance between Althusserian conceptions of the social formation and insights into the workings of ideology provided by Gramsci's (1971) theory of hegemony. Originally developed as a means by which to understand the process by which the dominant classes use their moral, political and intellectual leadership to establish their own world views as universal and all inclusive, hegemony identifies the provisional 'negotiated settlements' (Kellner, 1978) that arise throughout the 'the winning and shaping of consent so that the power of the dominating classes appears both legitimate and natural' (Hall, 1977).

The tradition of enquiry established by projects such as these was significant, therefore, in signalling the benefits that might come from cultural analyses which identified more precisely the social practices that characterize particular sites within the social formation, as well as the role of ideology in reproducing and transforming social relations. Subsequent research into the nature and effects of capitalist schooling was greatly influenced by insights such as these.

Class, Schooling and Social Reproduction

The research into American schooling by Bowles and Gintis (1976), for example, led them to explore more fully the relationship between practices in the educational and economic spheres of capitalist societies. Whilst their conclusion that 'the social relations of educational institutions correspond(ed) closely to the social relations of dominance, subordination and motivation in the economic sphere' came subsequently to be amended following criticisms that their work was 'economistic', 'functionalist' and insensitive to contradiction (Hogan, 1981; Apple, 1982), their book *Schooling in Capitalist America* was influential in establishing an agenda for later research into the role of schooling in processes of social reproduction and transformation.

The uneven and contradictory way in which schooling contributes to processes of cultural and social reproduction was more fully explored in Willis's (1977) classic study *Learning to Labour*. In this, he sought specifically to identify the forms of 'resistance' employed by a group of working class 'lads' in an English secondary school, and to relate these to central features within the dynamics of working class culture. In particular, he was able to show the way in which class culture affects the ways in which young people make sense of and respond to the culture of the school. Though Willis's study has sometimes been regarded as a celebration of working class 'resistance' to capitalist schooling, it is also deeply pessimistic in that, as its sub-title ('How Working Class Kids get Working Class Jobs') implies, it demonstrates how 'resistance' in school can serve to reproduce rather than transform existing social relations. Subsequently of course, Willis (1981) has claimed that neither of these interpretations is entirely in line with his theoretical position, which suggests that the significance of 'resistances' to schooling is not given, but depends upon how these are worked with, and how they articulate with other practices within the social formation.

Similar arguments were advanced in Gintis and Bowles' (1981) autocritique of the correspondence theory they developed in their early work. In analyzing the *constraints* imposed on the development of social practices within a particular site by virtue of that site's articulation with others, as well as the *possibilities* allowed for by the transportation of practices across sites, they advanced the view that determinate effects arise as an outcome of complex and contradictory articulations between practices at different sites within the social formation.

While studies like these did much to lay the foundations for the more sophisticated analyses of cultural and social reproduction that characterize work in the 1980s, by taking *class* as their central dynamic, they laid themselves open to subsequent claims that they were overly deterministic (Coward, 1977) as well as slanted in their marginalization of patriarchy as a critical determinant of the specificity of sub-cultural response (McRobbie and Garber, 1975; McRobbie, 1980).

The former of these two claims has, in retrospect, been shown to be the less serious of the two. Both theoretically (Chambers, Clarke, Connell, Curti, Hall and Jefferson, 1977; Willis, 1981 and 1982) and empirically (Hebdige, 1979), it has subsequently been demonstrated that the analytic frameworks developed throughout this period far from underestimated the innovative and socially transformative capacity of youth sub-cultural responses. Hebdige's (1979) analysis of Punk sub-culture, for example, attempted a more daring analysis than had hitherto been carried out of the processes of *signification* allowed for by youth sub-cultural responses as well as the *specific effectivity* of these practices in winning cultural space from more mainstream options. The second of these claims, however, requires more extended discussion since it highlights a series of problems with earlier materialist analyses of young people's school and sub-cultural behaviour which have only recently begun to be addressed.

Gender, Schooling and Social Reproduction

In her book *Women, Crime and Society*, Leonard (1985) points out that research into youth and youth sub-cultures has systematically marginalized the study of young women's experience. In discussing the work of the early sub-cultural theorists, for example, she points out that,

> ... Merton made no attempt to apply his typology to women ... Albert Cohen only discusses females briefly ... Cloward and Ohlin state that they will focus on males but never bother to explain why their situation differs from that of females ...

According to her analysis, similar omissions can also be found in the work of the 'new criminologists' whose efforts to derive a more fully *social* theory of deviance considerably influenced the research into youth sub-cultures carried out at the Centre for Contemporary Cultural Studies.

> ... Taylor, Walton and Young's massive criticism of criminology does not contain *one* word about women ...

Such systematic biases and conspicuous absences call for explanation, and it is in the male dominance of academic life that Heidensohn (1985) lays much of the blame. Of particular significance in this respect have been the pervasive 'ideologies of gender' which make it seem natural for many sociologists to look at men's behaviour and to ignore the actions of women. Similar ideas to these have been expressed by McRobbie (1980) in her critique of the research that was carried out into youth sub-cultures during the 1970s. According to her,

> ... If we look for the structured absences in the youth literature, it is the sphere of the family and domestic life that is missing. No commentary of the hippies dealt with the countercultural sexual division of labour, let alone the hypocrisies of 'free love', few writers seemed interested in what happened when a mod went home after a weekend on speed ...

In her critical re-reading of *Learning to Labour*, McRobbie argues that by over-emphasizing 'male pride in physical labour and contempt for "pen pushing"' and by focussing too closely on the 'cultural reproduction'of machismo from father to son', Willis (1977) marginalizes the effects of these processes for women's experience (both publically and within the home) and for the reproduction of gender relations. Similarly, Hebdige's (1979) analysis of sub-cultural meanings, whilst more sophisticated than previous attempts to do this, is flawed by its refusal to engage with questions of gender and sexuality.

In her own work, McRobbie (1978) more closely addresses issues such as these through an examination of the experience of a group of teenage working class girls. Whilst most of her fieldwork was carried out in a local youth club, McRobbie obtained limited information about what the girls she studied did at school. This showed that in contrast to middle class girls in the same school, who tended to be docile, diligent and conscientious ('swots' and 'snobs' as her respondents called them), the working class girls involved themselves in a wide variety of apparently oppositional activities. Many of these transformed the school,

> ... into the sphere, par excellence, for developing their social life, fancying boys, learning the latest dance, having a smoke together in the lavatory and playing up the teachers ...

According to McRobbie, such behaviour can only be understood in both class *and* gender terms. By 'resisting' the 'official, and middle class, ideology for girls in school (neatness, diligence, appliance, passivity) and by replacing this with a more feminine, even sexual, one', working class girls display both a class instinct and an awareness of the nature of gender oppression within school. In consequence, their behaviour affirms a culture of femininity which prizes highly 'finding a fella', 'attracting a steady' and 'getting married'. Their actions thereby simultaneously reproduce existing class *and* gender relations.

Similar themes to these can be found in the studies of Australian and North American schooling carried out by Connell, Ashenden, Kessler and Dowsett (1982) and Anyon (1983), respectively. The former study, in particular, reminds us of the need for a careful consideration of the relationship between home and school experience in making sense of students' responses at this latter site. Many of the actions that Connell and his co-workers document within the schools they studied, for example, have clear counterparts within the home. But Connell, Ashenden, Kessler and Dowsett's study is also important also in identifying the role played by students' school-based responses in more general processes of cultural and social reproduction, since it begins to identify more clearly how articulations between class and gender based practices within the school have consequences for the reproduction of *both* of these sets of relations.

In this respect, Anyon's (1983) work has also been valuable in alerting us to the relatedness of the processes within schools by which class and gender relations come to be reproduced. In her fieldwork amongst girls attending five elementary schools, for example, she identifies two dominant, but contradictory, ideologies of femininity confronting her respondents. The first of these (which is primarily working class in origin) emphasizes emotional passivity, nurturance and non-competitiveness. A second, more middle class, ideology places value on the display of confidence in school work and individual success in examinations. The extent to which young women experience the contradiction between those two ideologies, and the manner in which this contraction is resolved, varies according to the class location (and home experience) of the individual concerned. In consequence, and via processes which display both 'resistance' against and 'accommodation' within the power structures that organize school life, both class and gender relations are reproduced.

Both of these recent studies highlight the need for future research both to enquire more closely into the effects that arise when particular forms of class and gender experience are transported across different sites of experience. Similar themes emerged in MacDonald/Arnot's (1980, 1981a and 1981b) earlier analysis of the role of schooling in the reproduction of class and gender relations. In this, she shows how the formation of sexual identities within working class homes has important effects for the ways in which young people of different class backgrounds negotiate their school experience. In the case of working class boys, for example, she argues that the *recontextualization* at school of gender codes learned within the home has important consequences for the reproduction of class relations.

> ... Let us look for a moment at the distinction between mental and manual labour which is integral to the capitalist labour process. In bourgeois culture it is transposed with the hierarchy male over female — in other words mental labour is equated with the masculine and manual work or practical skills with the female. The dominant gender code within the school is likely to transmit this pairing of two hierarchies. However, as Willis has shown in *Learning to Labour*, working class boys confronted with this dual structure have two choices — either they conform, with the result that they lose credibility with their own class and deny their masculine sexuality or, they can

reject the message of the school. Significantly, the conformist or 'ear'ole' is labelled as effeminate or cissy . . .

For working class girls, on the other hand, the classification of mental work as male, and manual work as female poses less of a problem since this classification is one often reinforced within their family culture. The experience of middle class girls and middle class boys is, however, left relatively unexplored within the analytic framework which MacDonald/Arnot advocates.

In the light of the preceding comments, an adequate analysis of the processes by which class and gender relations come to be reproduced would seem to require a detailed exploration of social practices that take place in multiple sites. In particular, it would seem to require a detailed examination of the way in which class and gender practices are transported from site to site, and the effects of these transportations for the cultural reproduction of limiting forms of practice.

Conclusions

As was pointed out at the beginning of this chapter, educational and social scientific research has its origins in processes by which the topical concerns of researchers themselves are brought more closely into line with issues of debate within the relevant research literature. Throughout this chapter I have tried to show how this took place by identifying the research trajectory which is peculiar to the present enquiry.

In order to provide some degree of insight into the analysis which follows, it would seem useful at this point to summarize the major concerns which motivated the research carried out in this study. Of primary concern at the outset of this investigation into the nature and effects of modes of new middle class socialization, was a desire to understand more fully the processes by which a significant minority of young people from backgrounds high in cultural capital (Bourdieu and Passeron, 1977) come to 'underachieve' academically in GCE Advanced level examinations. Associated with this, was an interest in exploring more fully the processes of cultural production which take place at three relatively distinct sites of experience: domestically, educationally and sub-culturally.

Finally, and most significantly within the context of the research I have previously described, it seemed important to identify more adequately the effects of practices at these sites for processes of cultural and social reproduction. Ever since the emergence of the counter-cultures of the 1960s, there has been considerable debate about the extent to which the potential to transform society lies merely (or even mainly) with the traditional working class, as opposed to with (among others) disaffected professional and middle class groups (Roszak, 1968; Marcuse, 1969; Gintis, 1972). More recently, writers such as Anyon (1981a and 1981b), Giroux (1983), Giroux and Aronowitz (1986) and Whitty (1985) have, from varying perspectives, begun to identify the role of teachers in processes of social transformation. Anyon, in particular, has argued that it is possible to identify non-socially reproductive effects in both middle class and working class schools which can be worked upon by teachers to produce potentially transformative effects. According to her, by identifying and politicizing forms of 'penetrative practical understanding', which include 'cultural modes of resistance to oppressions and exploitations at school, at home, at work and by institutions of the media' (Anyon, 1981b), teachers can do much to enhance the revolutionary and transformative potential of student 'resistance' within schools. It, therefore, seemed to be of more than academic significance to enquire more closely into the nature of new middle class responses to schools and schooling.

The remainder of this book has been structured so as to address each of these concerns systematically. In chapter 2, I will describe how the students in the present study came to be selected and how fieldwork among them came to be carried out. In chapter 3, I will look more closely at social practices taking place within the homes in which students were resident. Chapters 4 and 5 detail the nature of respondents' educational and sub-cultural experience. Chapter 6 returns to a consideration of the implications of the practices described at these three sites for the more general processes by which class and gender relations come to be reproduced and transformed.

Chapter 2

Fieldwork

Introduction

So far, I have tried to identify the key commitments which I hoped to work with in making sense of the data collected in this study. A prior identification of these was necessary in order to distinguish a number of key analytic dimensions in a materialist analysis of new middle class household, educational and youth sub-cultural experience. However, it was also necessary in order to anticipate difficulties likely to be encountered in selecting respondents and in organizing fieldwork. In this chapter, I will describe how the students involved in this study were selected and how fieldwork among them came to be carried out.

Selecting the Group

Because of constraints on the research process imposed by time and resources, most forms of research have to investigate a small sample of individuals from within a wider population. The way in which selection takes place varies, however, according to the researcher's theoretical standpoint and the type of group under study. In general, large-scale sample surveys are carried out when high levels of reliability and population validity are being sought, whereas exploratory investigations which are stronger in ecological validity, are often conducted using ethnographic approaches to data collection and analysis (Bracht and Glass, 1968).

In most types of ethnography, the researcher's concern for homogeneity within the group being studied is likely to encourage the use of purposive sampling. Here, membership of the sample is structurally determined, and respondents are chosen because of relational characteristics they share. Two of the most frequently used forms of purposive sampling in ethnographic research are *expert choice* and *snowball* sampling (Smith 1975). The first of these involves the researcher, or some other 'expert', selecting individuals according to the extent to which they fit in with pre-specified research requirements. In the latter, the researcher builds up a group to be studied by asking an initial set of informants to supply the names of other potential sample members. Balanced against the possibility that in both cases generalization from sample to population is likely to be problematic, is the potential for in-depth study offered by a structurally defined group of individuals.

In this investigation, the decision was made to use a combination of different purposive sampling approaches in constituting a group of respondents for study. My own teaching experience at Spatown College had initially suggested the value of using college tutors as guides in a system of expert choice sampling. However, because informal observations before the fieldwork commenced had led me to believe that students following GCE Advanced level courses came from a variety of backgrounds, and because my particular research interest lay in exploring aspects of the educational experience of students from specifically new middle class homes, I felt it reasonable to further structure the sampling process.

A decision was therefore made to constitute an initial 'working universe' of respondents from those whose names had been mentioned in tutors' meetings throughout 1980 in connection with poor academic progress despite the fact that the individuals concerned came from homes high in cultural capital (Bourdieu and Passeron, 1977). Most of these students were, in fact, the daughters and sons of teachers, community workers and so on. To these names were then added those of other GCE Advanced level students in the college's Department of General Studies who were not so characterized. An aggregate list of twenty-eight names was then presented to each 'A' level tutor. The latter were then asked to comment confidentially on every student on the list, both in terms of their academic performance and with respect to the individual's perceived home and social life.

In order to enable tutors to respond in as idiosyncratic a way as possible, but also to facilitate a later comparison of responses *between* them, an approach to sampling based on Kelly's (1955) Personal Construct Theory (PCT) was adopted. Full details of the procedures involved are described elsewhere (Aggleton, 1984). In essence, however, they required tutors to first differentiate between students using constructs or dimensions of their own choice. Following this, tutors were asked to rate every student in the working universe of twenty-eight along each of these dimensions. These ratings were then subjected to a principal components analysis (Slater, 1972) in order to identify those students who tutors perceived as broadly similar to one another.

Techniques such as this have been used in a number of studies to identify clusters of individuals with similarly perceived characteristics. Ryle and Lipshitz (1974), for example, have used such a technique to investigate the ways in which psychiatric nurses construe patients in their care. Ryle and Lunghi (1968) and Rowe and Slater (1976) have also used PCT to explore changes in the perception of others following psychotherapeutic intervention. Past precedent therefore suggested the appropriateness of such a technique for investigating tutors' perceptions of students in this study. By subsequently comparing tutors' judgments it was possible to identify a *core cluster* of six students who were reliably distinguished from others undertaking GCE study in terms of criteria of research interest. These six students, who I shall call Brenda Miller, Pam Giles, Carol Smithson, Dave Lane, Elaine Scotwell and Wendy Stephens, were perceived by their tutors somewhat unusually, in that while they were rated highly in terms of academic *potential* and came from homes high in cultural capital, they were simultaneously judged as unlikely to do well in GCE Advanced level examinations. A more sophisticated appreciation of their social characteristics can be gained by looking more closely at some of the constructs used by tutors to differentiate this group from other students.

Mr Turner, a teacher of history of art, perceived these students as 'noisy and garulous in class', 'extrovert and unselfcontained'. Additionally, he saw them as 'unlikely to be persistent in their work', yet nevertheless 'very bright academically'. Finally, he thought it likely that the six students concerned might be seen 'drunk in the street in the evening'.

Mr Dickens, a teacher of English literature and communication studies differentiated these students from others in terms of a tendency to 'show off' in class and to be 'social performers in college'. He also perceived them to be 'socially alert in a political sense: left politically'. In talking about three of those concerned, he commented:

> ... Brenda, Wendy and Carol — they will end up in careers where their histrionic talent can be used to the full ... (*Mr Dickens*, Fieldnotes, 1980)

Mr Chamberlain, a teacher of history, aslo construed the six students in a similar way to one another, viewing them as 'academically able' but with 'an apparent unconcern for work'. Significantly, he also perceived them as likely to come from families which 'support their individuality and autonomy in decision-making'. He also believed them to be more 'fashion conscious' and 'sexually active' than many of their contemporaries at College.

The fourth tutor, Ms Weber, a teacher of social science, thought it likely that these six individuals came from 'unconventional homes', would be 'unlikely to get engaged or married in the near future' and were 'in the arty set at college in terms of clothes and appearance'. She too felt it unlikely that they would 'do well in 'A' level examinations'.

Mr Stoppard, a teacher of English and theatre studies, also felt that the students concerned would be unlikely to 'work well under pressure' or 'get good 'A' level grades'. Additionally, he saw them as 'extrovert in class', 'very communicative about irrelevant matters (to work)' and 'politically involved'. In the course of his description of Pam Giles, for example, he remarked:

> ... She's loud and noisy and tries to take over the establishment. Often in class she has this disarming approach of saying in a loud voice, 'I don't understand this.' She's faintly dramatic ... (*Mr Becket*, Fieldnotes, 1980)

When asked to explain such behaviour, Mr Becket was able to identify connections between this and qualities which he felt were likely to be true of students' home life:

> ... They give you the feeling that they come from too liberal a background. Therefore, they lack the application and diligence which, with intelligence, makes you a success in our society. Wendy once said to me when she arrived late for class, 'Well, you've got to understand that I come from a very liberal family. That's why I can't get up for college in the morning. My parents don't mind, so why should you?' ... (*Mr Becket*, Fieldnotes, 1980)

The final tutor interviewed, Ms Bronte, a teacher of English literature, also felt that the six students were broadly similar to one another in terms of their academic 'potential' and lack of 'work commitment'. Her ratings differed from those of other tutors, however, in that there seemed little other evidence of consistency within them. In view of the idiographic nature of PCT and its concern to remain faithful to the individuality of human perception, it is perhaps not surprising that perfect consistency between tutors' perceptions was not attained. Nevertheless, from the analysis presented above, it is possible to identify a number of key qualities characterizing this group of students.

First, they were perceived as extrovert in College, being likely to contribute with little prompting to tutor-led discussions. Second, their attendance at class was something which could not be relied on. Third, these students were seen as individuals who would be unlikely to work consistently in the pursuit of academic goals. Finally, a number of tutors drew connections between these types of behaviour and aspects of students' home lives. In particular, it was felt that their failure to acquire attitudes and behaviour conducive to academic success could be related to parental encouragement of high levels of personal autonomy in decision making within the home.

Using this core group of six students as a starting point, the remainder were sampled on the basis of friendship with one or more members of this group and registration for GCE Advanced level study at Spatown College. On such a basis it was possible to constitute a group of twenty-seven respondents in total who, because of sibling relationships amongst them, came from a total of twenty households. Details of the individuals concerned, and their residence at the time of the fieldwork, are to be found in appendices 1 and 2. A summary description of the information in these appendices is provided in tables 1 and 2. Overall, seventeen respondents were the children of teachers in primary, secondary, further or higher education. Of those remaining, a further seven came from households where one or both adult members worked in the creative, mediated or theatre arts.

Students in this study were therefore relatively homogeneous in terms of their social background. All came from homes which could be characterized as new middle class using frameworks suggested by class theorists as diverse as Poulantzas (1975), Ehrenreich and Ehrenreich (1979), Wright (1980) and Bernstein (1977). Moreover, within this broad category, the majority of respondents came from backgrounds where the work of one or both parents was that associated with processes of symbolic control.

Beginning Fieldwork

When beginning ethnographic fieldwork, McCall and Simmons (1969) argue that attention should be given to the nature of the researcher's field-role. In this study, I initially decided to adopt a

Table 1: Occupational status of students' parents (thirty-seven alive at the time of the fieldwork)

Teacher in primary or secondary education	8
Teacher in further or higher education	11
Actors/community artists	4
Painter/designer	3
Owner of small business	4
Others	7

Table 2: Class location of students' households by theorist (total of twenty households investigated

Theorist	Class	Number of households
Ehrenreich and Ehrenreich (1979)	Professional and managerial class	18
	Petit Bourgeoisie	2
Bernstein (1977)	Agents of symbolic control	19
	Working class/indeterminate	1
Poulantzas (1975)	New Petit Bourgeoisie (fraction 2)	17
	Traditional Petit Bourgeoisie	3
Carchedi (1977 and 1983)	Old middle class	3
	New middle class	5
	Working class	12
Wright (1978 and 1980)	Semi-autonomous employees	16
	Managers and supervisors	1
	Petit Bourgeoisie	1
	Self-employed	2

field-role incorporating aspects of Gold's (1958) first two ideal-typical strategies: complete participation and participation with observation. Only by doing this did I feel it would be possible to access the meanings and understandings underlying respondents' day-to-day activities.

To some extent, the adoption of a field strategy intermediate between these two roles was helped by prior familiarity on my part with contexts in which respondents spent their time. Before beginning the major part of the fieldwork, but after identifying the core cluster of respondents previously described. I spent several months exploring the social and spatial contexts frequented by students following GCE Advanced level courses at Spatown College. While doing this, and in order to enhance the naturalism of the study, I presented a particular rationale for my research interest.

It first became necessary to think about this some three or four months before the main body of fieldwork commenced. After my application for unpaid leave of absence had been formally approved by the governors of Spatown College, a number of teaching colleagues mentioned in class that I would shortly be leaving. Following this, several students asked me directly what I would be doing once I had gone and who would take over the teaching of classes I had previously taught. Because of this, it was in some ways fortuitous that I had not explained in detail to teaching colleagues what the research was likely to involve. Some were of the belief that I was vaguely interested in youth culture. Others, in line with a prevalent attitude in the College at that time towards staff involvement in in-service training, thought I would be taking it easy for a year or so at the local University. On the few occasions when I was asked more directly what the work would involve, I intimated that my interest lay in exploring why some students studied GCE Advanced level subjects in colleges of further education rather than at school. In response to questions from students about my imminent departure, I therefore decided to extend the use of this justification to them.

Away from College, however, I was concerned to develop a field-role which would facilitate data collection over the coming months. In particular, my interest lay in cultivating what Lofland (1971) has called an air of *acceptable incompetence*. Because many of the students in whom I was interested spent much of their time away from College talking about problems coping with their courses, I adopted such a role, presenting myself as disillusioned with teaching, but interested in finding out why so many students at Spatown College performed relatively unsuccessfully in their GCE examinations. As time passed, I elaborated upon this account to suggest that I had been working on such a project for some time, but with relatively little success, prior to giving up teaching altogether.

Negotiating Entry to the Field

Ethnography generally requires the investigator to infiltrate and enter a research context in a controlled way. In this study, where the decision had already been made to investigate aspects of students' home, educational and sub-cultural experience, I thought it appropriate to enter the field at two different levels: exploring simultaneously, aspects of students' home and sub-cultural lives. This decision was made partly in order to delay detailed enquiry into students' educational experience until I felt confident that I would no longer be perceived as a member of Spatown College's staff, but also because preliminary observations suggested that some aspects of respondents' sub-cultural experience and some domestic situations would be easier to gain access to than others.

Consequently, the decision was made to approach one particular member of the core group of students previously identified at the same time as access was sought to the homes of others. The first of these objectives was accomplished by arranging a meeting with Dave Lane, a student I had previously taught. Dave had failed all of the GCE Advanced level examinations he had taken the previous year at College and was living at home unemployed at this time. Before this meeting, he and I had talked briefly a few times in the street and in 'The Roundhouse', one of the public houses frequented by College students. However, we had never met in isolation. After telephoning Dave and finding that he was keen to talk, we agreed to meet in one of the bars at the 'Tattered Pheasant', a public house popular with both College students and members of Spatown's well-established hippie community. As it turned out, he had already heard that I had given up teaching and we spent the remainder of the evening talking before moving at Dave's suggestion to the 'Dugout', a late-night drinking club.

My second objective, which involved gaining access to the households in which students lived, was accomplished rather less deliberately. One evening, after rehearsing for an amateur production of Anouihl's play *Antigone*, I met Brenda Miller's father, a lecturer in French literature at the local University. We were later joined by his wife who had just returned from a Management Committee meeting at Spatown Youth Centre. In addition to her involvement in voluntary youth work, Mrs Miller was an Student Welfare Officer at the local College of Art. Knowing that Brenda and a number of other students had been very involved with the Youth Theatre operating at Spatown Youth Centre, I began talking with Mrs Miller about current activities there. In the course of this conversation, I was asked whether I would be interested in standing for the position of Treasurer on the Centre's Management Committee. I agreed, and following my election, arrangements were made for me to call round at the Millers' household for me to be briefed on what this position would involve. Through my connection with Spatown Youth Centre, it was subsequently possible to make contact with the parents of other members of the core group of students earlier identified, many of whom, as it happened, were also involved in amateur dramatic and operatic productions staged at the centre. As a result, I was invited to a number of meetings and social gatherings on subsequent evenings and it proved possible to extend my fieldwork to include many of the households concerned.

Having gained entry to the field on these two rather different levels, I set about exploring each of them systematically. Initially, I focussed my concern on the lives of students themselves and on snowballing a sufficiently large group of respondents for the study. After meeting Dave again on several occasions, and talking more extensively with him about his reasons for attending College as well as about what he had done since leaving, I suggested that I was interested in meeting others like him. As a result, he suggested the names of three other people I should talk to, who fortunately were also members of the core cluster of potential respondents identified by my earlier analysis of tutors' ratings. He subsequently arranged for me to meet one of them, Sarah, who was his girlfriend at the time. From this point on, a considerable amount of time was spent progressively building up the final group of respondents.

Establishing the Field Role

Having successfully negotiated entry to the field, it became essential to consider various aspects of the field role I intended to adopt. According to Douglas (1976), the field researcher should,

> ... try to be liked first, and on that he can build powerful bonds of trust. If he isn't liked, it won't matter whether he's trusted — he won't penetrate to the inner depth of things ...

In aiming to increase the likelihood that I would be accepted in this way, I tried to be as egalitarian and sociable as possible. To some extent, this was helped by the fact that when fieldwork began I honestly knew little about the reality of students' lives away from college or, indeed, about their reasons for studying there. However, while considerable effort was put into creating a relatively egalitarian relationship between myself and the students, maintaining this was something which had continuously to be struggled for. It became clear, for example, that from time to time students would ask questions encouraging me to re-adopt the role of teacher or expert. Comments inviting my views on issues as disparate as local politics, existentialism and herbal medicine were made with some regularity in early group discussions to which I was party. These required careful handling if I was to avoid presenting myself as some kind of an authority. Initially, I indicated that I did not really know the answers to questions such as these. Later in the fieldwork, I learned to avoid eye contact when I felt such questions were about to be asked. On the few occasions when it proved difficult to avoid making responses implying a greater knowledge on my part, I tried always to preface my remarks with statements of uncertainty.

Sociability was also aimed for in a variety of ways. For much of the time this meant being available whenever students wanted to be with me. I therefore turned down as few invitations to go out as possible and, when with respondents, tried quickly to detect events in which interest and amusement were shown. On the whole, this proved to be an effective strategy. However, particular problems were encountered with respect to my involvement in one particular type of discussion which occupied much of the students' time. This took the form of debate and gossip about what friends and other people were 'really like'. Since a great deal of time seemed to be spent talking about others in this way, it was difficult for me to avoid joining in if I was to be considered a bona fide member of the group. However, to do so created the possibility that I might be regarded as untrustworthy. Indeed, as it emerged later, those students who most involved themselves in this type of discussion were perceived in exactly this way by the others. Fortunately, early in the fieldwork I had observed that a few respondents seemed able to get away with saying little about others. They would recount in a matter of fact way what they knew other people had done, but would rarely offer judgment on these actions. In consequence I aimed to reveal as little as possible to respondents about others in the group and when this proved absolutely unavoidable, I tried to do so in ways which were relatively devoid of evaluation.

A significant threat to the establishment of egalitarian and sociable relationships between students and myself came from my own higher level of personal income. It had been my intention from the start to avoid being seen by respondents as a financial benefactor and while the danger of this had been reduced by the fact that my leave of absence from College was unpaid, it took some time to adjust my social patterns of expenditure to those of students.

Eliciting information from respondents was at times a delicate process since, initially, I did not initially want to reveal my interest in the relationship between class location, educational attainment and sub-cultural activity. There were several reasons for this. First, I felt it would be difficult to explain such concerns in ways which would be readily comprehensible to respondents. Second, I felt it unwise to make reference to academic 'underachievement' early in the fieldwork, at a time when I was attempting to establish relatively egalitarian relationships, since to do so could have aroused unhelpful memories of me as a college teacher. Finally, I did not want to talk openly about sub-cultural style at this stage in the research since doing this might have influenced how respondents saw themselves.

While it was clear that students socially differentiated themselves from others of comparable age in Spatown, on the whole this was done negatively in terms of what they were *not*, rather than positively in terms of what they were. Thus, respondents took great care to differentiate themselves from 'hippie types' (who were perceived as dirty and lazy), 'straights' (those in full-time employment who bought their clothes in 'High Street' shops and frequented Spatown's largest commercial discotheque) and other, more obvious, groups such as skinheads and punks. However, more positive forms of self-identification were rarely used.

By avoiding the use of terms such as 'sub-culture' and 'style' in the account I gave of my research interests, I hoped to avoid any premature self-typification by respondents. In consequence, I offered as the major rationale for my research, an interest in why some people choose to study GCE Advanced level subjects at a college of further education. Such strategies, or ploys of indirection as Douglas (1976) has called them, have a valuable role to play in reducing reactivity to researchers and their interests.

Field Mapping

After gaining access to the field, it is important to begin to identify regularities within it in order to allow a systematic approach to data collection. Such a process of *field mapping* is likely to require the researcher to focus on aspects of what Schatzman and Strauss (1973) have called the spatial, social and temporal contexts of individual and group behaviour.

The Social Map

Social mapping is a process which attempts to chart significant features of the social relationships which respondents enter into. In constructing the social map of a particular research setting, an ethnographer is likely to record the number and variety of persons present, the hierarchical nature (or otherwise) of relationships between them and the division of labour to which they conform. In this study, preliminary information relevant to these concerns had already been obtained from the earlier analysis of tutors' ratings, since these had enabled the identification of a relatively homogeneous group of students united both by course membership and by friendship and association. Initial fieldwork, however, revealed the existence of further significant social dimensions within students' experience. For example, seventeen of the final group of respondents lived in homes where one or both heads of household were teachers in primary, secondary, further or higher education. Moreover, eleven of the households studied were headed by single parents — in all but one case, women.

Social relations in these households had a number of distinctive qualities to them. The most obvious of these related to the near constant stream of visitors calling in throughout the day. Compared with traditional working class or managerial middle class homes, there seemed little sense that these households were essentially private domains to be protected from the gaze of outsiders. Friends, neighbours and acquaintances were forever arriving unexpectedly, to sit for hours talking and drinking coffee in the large kitchen/living areas which most homes had. Indeed, such visiting took place even when those normally resident in the household were not themselves present, with callers letting themselves in through rarely locked front-doors and making themselves at home until the former returned. To some extent, this flow of visitors was encouraged by the fact that many households rented rooms to students from the local University and Polytechnic, and to artists and those working in media and theatre arts. The existence of this significant dimension to respondents' home life had the fortunate consequence of enabling me to gain access on several occasions to each of the households concerned.

A final feature of the social map worthy of note, concerned the existence of a small number of students who, at the time of the fieldwork, were resident away from home in flats or bedsits. Susan Turner and Wanda Wilson, for example, both lived in rented flats and sub-let parts of these to other members of the group throughout the study. As will be seen, the existence of such settings, away from direct parental surveillance, was to add a significant dimension to students' sub-cultural experience.

The Spatial Map

The spatial mapping of a research context aims to identify critical socializing contexts within it. In the present study, five such settings were identified and fieldwork was carried out in each of these. In broad terms, these five contexts can be described as public houses, nightclubs, public meeting places such as cafes and art centres, places of work and homes themselves. Of these, places of work and public meeting places were to a large extent synonymous since thirteen respondents worked part-time in cafes and restaurants and would meet there with friends either during or after work. A sixth setting was also identified: this was Spatown College itself. However, in order to minimize possible reactivity arising from students' past memories of me as a teacher, the decision was made to collect data relating to this particular context through retrospective accounts given by students rather than by direct observation.

Public houses

There were over 100 public houses in Spatown at the time of the fieldwork, of which about twenty were in the centre of the city. However, only a few of these were regularly frequented by the students. One public house in particular, 'The Roundhouse', was very popular and had been regularly used by respondents for some years. In part, its popularity stemmed from the fact that the landlord seemed relatively unconcerned about the age of his clientele.

> ... Why did you go there all the time? (PA)
> ... Well, I suppose it might have had something to do with the landlord. I mean, there must only be some landlords who will put up with obviously underage drinkers. Besides, we'd been going there since we were at school ... (*Wendy*, Interview, March 1981)

There were other reasons too why 'The Roundhouse' was a popular meeting place. Some of these related to the kinds of people likely to be met there.

> ... Why did you go to 'The Roundhouse' so much? (PA)
> ... (I went there) because it was full of people that I knew. It was full of the crowd that I was with at the time and I liked going there, talking with people that I knew. All the people from College and some from school and all that. I mean, you

have to have a meeting place don't you? ... (*Brenda*, Interview, December 1980)

Other reasons related to the kind of people who would be *unlike-*ly to be found there. Indeed, respondents' preference for this particular context and others close by such as 'The Crown' and 'The Tattered Pheasant' seemed also to be connected with a dislike of other public houses in Spatown, particularly those such as 'The Victorian' which were popular with young people of a comparable age to students, but in full-time employment.

> ... Would you ever go to 'The Victorian'? (PA)
> ... God no, that's where the disco trendies go. It's so funny, I went in there recently. It was full of people with baggy jeans and T shirts. It's odd ... (*Ric*, Interview, September 1981)

> ... Did you ever go to 'The Victorian'? (PA)
> ... We went to 'The Victorian' when we were about 14. Checked trousers and high-heeled shoes. We were proper little trendies then. We were 14 and used to go in the pub and drink gin and tonics. We used to wear hairspray and lipstick and eyeliner and blusher and foundation cream ... (*Norma* Interview, December 1980)

Preferred public houses could be distinguished from others not only by their clientele but also by their location. Both 'The Roundhouse' and 'The Crown' occupied imposing Georgian premises in the centre of Spatown, close to antique and second-hand clothes shops, whole food stores and premises occupied by community theatre groups and arts associations.

Clubs

At the time of the fieldwork there were six nightclubs in Spatown and ten bars with late-night licences. Some of these locations were popular with students whereas others were regarded with varying degrees of antipathy. Discotheques managed by corporate leisure chains were particularly unpopular among respondents, many of whom claimed to have outgrown what they had to offer.

> ... I mean, I was going to places like the Mecca when I was 14. I wouldn't go there now. The men we used to go with were bricklayers and people like that ... really noisy and crude ... (*Wendy*, Interview, March 1981)

> ... Well I don't think discos like that are much fun really. I mean, they're just like cattle markets really I think. The women are all wearing pretty dresses and the men are up at the bar getting pissed. And then there's a nice little dance to *Boney M* or something like that. And I've never been able to see what they're for really. And all those straight people. Uck ... (*Carol*, Interview, May 1981)

More positively evaluated clubs were those frequented by students from local institutions of higher education. 'Snoopy's', a privately owned discotheque and 'The Dugout', a late-night drinking club were particularly popular. Later on, however, 'The Tube', a club used by members of Spatown's gay community, came to be a major focus of activity.

Homes

Social mapping has already distinguished between students resident at home throughout the fieldwork and those living independently in flats and bedsits. Marked similarities existed, however, between both of these contexts in terms of what took place within them. In particular, in each there was a conspicuous flow of visitors throughout the day, as friends, acquaintances and those just passing by called in, to talk, drink coffee or simply to pass the time. Considerable pride seemed to be taken in the numbers of those visiting.

> ... That was when I was doing my Youth Theatre bit and everyone used to come round to our house all the time. There was never an evening when there were less than five people there. But that was when we were doing our social bit you know. We were having parties all the time and people were always coming back late ... (*Jill*, Interview, September 1981)

In all cases, the head of the household concerned also took pleasure in the existence of this type of activity. Sometimes friends of students would stay overnight or for periods of several days or more. Furthermore, within a short space of time I too was encouraged to call in regularly at many of the homes involved.

> ... You must come round and meet Barbara's father. He's really incredible. He used to be a philosophy lecturer at the University but gave all that up because it was becoming too much. You can just drop by any evening. There's always people there in the kitchen, just talking about things. There's

food and this really lethal home brew. It's best after the pub's shut ... (*Robin*, Fieldnotes, July 1981)

Because of this, data collection in each of the households proved to be far from the difficult task which I had earlier anticipated.

Public meeting places and places of work

These two aspects of the spatial map will be described together because for students they were to a large extent synonymous. Four places in particular were popular either as sources of part-time employment or as contexts in which to meet. These were Spatown Arts Centre, 'Uncle Sam's' and 'The Alice in Wonderland' (two relatively inexpensive burger restaurants) and 'Pizza Paradise'.

Spatown Arts Centre was a cultural centre situated in the centre of the city. Throughout the day its spacious hall was used as a restaurant and coffee shop serving a variety moussaka-like dishes, quiches and wholefood salads. In the evening alternative theatre and mime groups occasionally performed but more often the space would be used for screenings of European art house films. The Arts Centre was a popular location with students who would sit for hours on its brightly coloured sofas drinking the occasional cup of coffee. Since little pressure was exerted on customers to buy food, literally hours could be spent talking in this particular setting.

'The Alice in Wonderland' and 'Pizza Paradise' were restaurants well patronized by students from the local University, Polytechnic and Art College. They were also places where customers were not expected to order from a set menu. It was therefore not unusual to find customers eating only ice-cream or perhaps drinking wine alongside those who had ordered more substantial meals. All had cocktail bars in which it was possible to drink either before and after eating or, once your face was known, without ordering food at all. Both of these restaurants were staffed predominantly by students from Spatown College undertaking part-time work concurrent with their GCE study.

'Uncle Sam's' was even less formal than the two restaurants so far described, being for a time staffed entirely by the students involved in the present study. As one of them remarked,

... The customers there got their hamburgers if they were lucky. I mean, the needle between the chefs and the waiters was incredible. If you got inefficient chefs and inefficient waiters then you'd end up with customers half way to the door before they got their food ... (*Dave*, Interview, February 1981)

As it happened, 'Uncle Sam's' closed a year after opening, reputedly as a result of its having made substantial trading losses. Nevertheless, throughout its limited time of opening it was very popular with respondents who used it as a meeting place as well as a source of part-time employment.

A significant feature of the contexts so far described was the relatively unclear distinction drawn between those working in them and those who were customers. For example, staff wore their normal everyday clothes at work, and being well-known as a regular customer facilitated the chance of subsequently being offered employment. Furthermore, all were locations used by students for celebrations such as birthday parties. The nature of these occasions frequently caused consternation to other customers, since chefs and waiting staff would frequently leave their other duties to sit for lengthy periods drinking wine and talking with their friends.

The Temporal Map

In constructing a temporal map of a research context, ethnographers look for schedules of work and leisure governing the use of particular interactional contexts. By identifying these, the researcher is likely to be able to organize fieldwork in such a way as to allow for periods of critical reflection on what has been discovered. Moreover, temporal mapping can also allow the identification of *critical incidents* in the social activities of those being studied.

In this study, I set about constructing a temporal map by first charting the way in which settings such as communal meeting places, public houses and clubs were used in the late afternoon and evening. Carrying out this task was, in part, facilitated by my own prior acquaintance with some of these contexts. Having gained information relevant to each of these situations, I then extended the fieldwork to explore the ebb and flow of social activity in homes and flats. My access to these settings was negotiated initially through my involvement in community theatre projects or after evenings spent in the company of students. It eventually proved possible to gain access to homes during earlier parts of the day as well. On some occasions, this was in connection with my interest in community arts, but on others it was as a result of my adopting a strategy learned from students themselves: that of dropping by while 'just passing'. Access to homes during the early morning proved the most difficult to gain since this was a period of time when access seemed to be granted primarily to family members or sexual intimates. Information relating to this time of day had therefore to be collected largely through retrospective accounts provided by students themselves. Temporal mapping of this type enabled further detail to be added to my overall understanding of the social practices of students and those with whom they lived.

I have already pointed out that a prevalent set of activities among those investigated was inter-household visiting. Temporal mapping during the early stages of fieldwork, however, enabled a clearer identification of times during the day when this was most likely to take place. In particular, the periods from about 4.00 in the afternoon until 8.00 in the evening, and from the time when public houses closed until 1.00 in the morning seemed to be those most occupied by this type of activity. In contrast, students tended to spend the morning sleeping-in and generally recovering from the exertions of the night before, with the consequence that morning classes at College tended to be irregularly attended.

Identifying temporal patterns such as these played a vital role in enabling me to develop an better appreciation of the ebb and flow of interaction within the group. It also allowed me to identify times in the day when I could temporarily withdraw from the field in order to write up fieldnotes and reflect on what I had been part of.

Whilst constructing the temporal map, it also became clear that after students had arrived at College they would frequently leave it between classes, returning throughout the day to their own homes or those of friends. Depending on what subsequently transpired, a decision would be made whether or not to return to College later in the day. In consequence, attendance at College came to be, for the most part, sporadic and relatively uncommitted.

Another temporal feature of interest concerned the timing and circumstances of meals within students' homes. Only rarely did members of a particular household eat together. Students frequently prepared their own food and ate when parents were absent or after they themselves had returned home from visiting friends late in the evening. In a number of households, food was regularly reheated throughout the course of an evening as different household members returned.

The identification of critical moments in patterns of social activity, occasions on which there is an intensification of communication and interaction, can play a useful role in alerting researchers to the existence of incidents of crucial significance for a particular group. Research among students revealed the existence of three, rather different, types of *critical incident*. The first of these took the form of parties and planned social gatherings in the home. Two rather different types of party were readily identifiable. The first of these were occasions on which students and their parents, as well as friends of both of these groups, were likely to be present. Parties of this type took place with some regularity, coinciding with birthdays and seasonal celebrations. They tended to be 'open-house' events, beginning perhaps at lunch-time and continuing until the early hours of the following day. A basic supply of food and alcoholic drink would be provided by those normally resident in the household, to which those invited would be expected to add. Generally speaking, the entire house would be given over to such parties, with people of all ages relating to each other with apparent ease and familiarity.

As fieldwork progressed, however, it became possible to distinguish a second type of party, one rather different in form from that just described. Parties of this latter type typically took place when parents were away from home, either overnight or on holiday. On these occasions, there was relatively little by way of advance preparation, with the party commencing late at night after public houses had closed. Those invited would bring with them relatively large amounts of alcoholic drink as well as drugs such as marijuana and amphetamines. Once again, most of the house would be given over to the event, with upstairs as well as downstairs rooms being used for dancing, smoking (marijuana) and sexual activity. Usually the bathroom and toilet would be occupied more or less continuously throughout the evening by guests being sick, crying over crises in interpersonal relationships, threatening suicide and so on.

Arguments and crises in personal relationships were not, of course, confined to parties, and since the events precipitating these can reveal much about the principles on which established relationships are maintained, it was important to focus my fieldwork on this second type of critical moment. In doing this, care was taken to identify factors preceding, accompanying and following arguments and conflicts. Initially, this was done by means of observation and by analyzing accounts given retrospectively by those involved. In the later stages of the fieldwork, however, I was afforded a more privileged role with respect to such events when respondents called on me at home, often without advance warning and in the early hours of the morning, to discuss recent interpersonal crises. While a readiness to do this may be taken as a measure of the degree of trust established between students and myself, these visits were to create a considerable degree of role conflict for myself as a researcher. Although I took great care not to reveal to others the names of those who had called round, or the pretext for this, I was often asked about this subsequently. Respecting the confidence of those who used me in this way proved difficult in the face of such questioning, but it was something which I worked hard to do.

A final set of critical incidents took the form of vacational reunions between students and friends who had moved away from Spatown. Two Easter holidays, two Christmas holidays and two summer vacations served as foci for research activity between the time when fieldwork began in 1980 and finished some two-and-a-half years later. These were occasions which were used to keep up to date on significant events elsewhere and were characterized by an intensification of visiting and interaction between respondents.

Data Collection

> ... To exert maximum control over ... experience, the re-searcher requires an efficient system for recording it. What the researcher requires are recording tactics which will provide ... an ongoing, developmental dialogue between (the role of) discoverer and social analyst ... (Schatzman and Strauss, 1973)

The most frequently employed technique for recording data ethnographically involves the taking of fieldnotes. Sometimes these may be made in the presence of those being studied, but more often they are likely to be written-up during periods of contemplation and reflection once a researcher has temporarily withdrawn from the field. In this study, the decision was made not to write detailed fieldnotes in the presence of members of the group being studied, since it was felt that this might present an undue threat to the naturalism of the enquiry. Instead, I decided to prepare a detailed record of events at the end of each day from key phrases and descriptions noted earlier. On the whole, such an approach worked relatively successfully, since critical aspects of the temporal map of the research setting tended to occur in the afternoon and evening. However, on a number of occasions it was necessary to momentarily leave the immediate research context for the privacy of an empty room to write down key comments which could act as triggers for the subsequent preparation of fieldnotes. On other occasions, after returning home I used a tape-recorder to dictate a record of incidents which had taken place during the day.

In addition to collecting data in these ways, each respondent was interviewed informally. This was felt necessary after it became clear that, for some students at least, there was some discrepancy between the attitudes and opinions they publicly expressed amongst friends and those they shared more privately with me. Such statements and behaviours, suggesting a degree of contradiction within respondents' social practice, were of considerable interest ethnographically since they provided insight into the multiple perspectives underpinning respondents' social action. It was important to explore tensions between these in order to do justice to the complexity of patterns of subjectivity and practice amongst this particular group of students. In consequence, every student was also informally interviewed after efforts had first been made to gain the confidence and trust of the person concerned. In the majority of cases, these informal interviews took place towards the middle of the fieldwork in either the student's or my own home, this latter context having by this point become a familiar setting for those involved.

Throughout the study, none of the students refused this request. Indeed, many seemed pleased that I was interested in talking with them about this. During the course of a two-to-three-hour semi-structured interview, it was possible to explore students' perceptions of their home life, the nature of their education prior to and while at Spatown College, and their social and cultural interests. Additionally, data was collected about how I myself was perceived by members of the group in order to facilitate a more reflexive interpretation of the research findings. The interview schedule used was a flexible one which identified in general terms a range of key issues to be explored without specifying a fixed order in which to do this (appendix 3). The schedule was committed to memory before the interviews were carried out and a relatively unobtrusive micro-recorder was used to record the data collected. Respondents were told in advance that they could stop the tape at any time or erase any material which they did not wish to be used. In fact, none of them exercised this option.

Checking Accounts

It is fundamental in ethnographic enquiry for the researcher to attempt an assessment of the validity of accounts given by respondents. This is important for a number of reasons. First of all, respondents may distort their descriptions of events because of expectations they hold about the researcher's interests and intentions. In doing this, they may describe things which never happened, make attributions which they would not otherwise hold and exaggerate that which is partially true.

To some extent I had hoped to minimize the danger of bias of this kind by offering what I hoped would be a plausible account of my own research interests. Furthermore, by immersing myself in the research situation after a period of prior acclimatization, I hoped to establish a secure foundation of direct experience on which to draw in detecting the more obvious evasions and deceptions that students might employ. (Douglas, 1976). In order to build up this fund of knowledge, I turned down invitations to be with respondents as rarely as could be avoided. For some time, therefore, my social life independent of the research context became almost non-existent. Friends of mine commented about being unable to locate me for days on end, the telephone went unanswered and bills went unpaid.

This first strategy, by which I hoped to make some assessment of the validity of the data collected, was closely linked to another by which I aimed to use alternative accounts to check the veracity of statements made in my presence. By comparing the accounts of events and actions given by individuals to different audiences, it is possible to identify not only the features common to all of them, but also the degree of variation within them. Since many of the situations described by respondents were those which had been collectively experienced both by myself and others, this proved a useful strategy to adopt in checking both the accuracy of accounts given and the range of interpretations offered.

Conclusions

In this chapter I have described how the students in this study were selected. I have also identified in general terms a number of features characterizing the ethnographic fieldwork which I carried out. In the next three chapters, I will move to a more detailed consideration of the patterns of practice identified in each of three key experiential contexts for students — within the home, educationally and sub-culturally. The first of these sites identifies the setting in which respondents were resident at the time of the research. The second, aims to distinguish contexts in which formal educational experience had been offered. The third highlights a sphere of practice relatively hidden from parental and teacherly surveillance. Each of these sites will

be examined separately before an attempt is made to identify resonances and tensions between the practices documented at each of
them.

Chapter 3

Home

Introduction

Recent work in the sociology of education, focussing on processes of cultural and social reproduction (Willis, 1977; MacDonald/Arnot, 1980; Connell, Ashenden, Kessler and Dowsett, 1982), has emphasized the need to consider the relationship between home, educational and sub-cultural experience in accounting for particular educational outcomes and modes of stylistic expression. By doing this, it may be possible to better understand the role played by articulations between sets of social practices across sites of experience, in reproducing and transforming social relations. In this chapter, therefore, attention will be focussed on social practices characterizing one of these three sites, before the relationship between these and those in other contexts is more closely identified.

Household Structures

Twenty households in total were visited during the course of the fieldwork and detailed observations were made in each of these on several occasions. The major demographic and social characteristics of these homes are described in appendix 1. Each of the twenty household units was resident in accommodation dating from the turn of the century or before. Seven of them occupied houses originally built in the eighteenth century, twelve lived in houses built in the nineteenth century and one was resident in early twentieth century accommodation. All lived in what were, without exception, substantial properties likely to retail at the upper end of Spatown's housing market. Few would have fetched less than £50,000 on the open market in 1982. Of these homes, fourteen had been purchased some fifteen to twenty years earlier when they had been in a state of relative disrepair. Most had undergone subsequent modernization by their owners and all were physically large with an average of 4.6 bedrooms in each. In part, their size could be accounted for in terms of average household size which was 3.4 children. However, since the siblings of many students were no longer resident at home when the fieldwork was carried out, spare bedrooms were to be found in most of them. Of the twenty households studied, ten were headed by parents who were single as a result of divorce or separation. Only one of these was headed by a man.

Foreshadowed Problems

In the previous chapter, it was argued that ethnography invariably takes place against a background of sensitizing concepts and theoretical commitments which take their origin from existing research. By forging links between these and the more topical categories and practices witnessed in the field, ethnographers attempt to construct new generic conceptualizations of theoretical utility.

Sensitizing my own investigation of students' home lives were a number of such sets of understandings. In particular, the work of Rapoport and Rapoport (1976) among middle class 'dual-career' families, played an important role in alerting me to the importance of investigating the division of labour within new middle class homes such as these. Their suggestion that it is largely the taking in of students, lodgers and paid helpers undertaking essential domestic labour which allows members of such households to spend proportionately large amounts of time travelling, entertaining and visiting, provided an initial source of impetus for enquiry.

My study of students' homes was also influenced by the work of Eiduson, Kornefin, Zimmerman and Weisner (1982) in the United States. In analyzing patterns of socialization in new middle class single parent, 'social contract' and communal-living families, they discovered the existence of a dominant type of socialization in many of these which emphasized the value of association with non-biologically related others (both adults and children), the development of personal autonomy in decision-making and the value of overt reasoning in processes of parental control. Since preliminary observations within the households involved in this study had suggested the presence of similar patterns of socialization within them too, it was felt important to explore the nature and consequences of these in some detail.

More significantly, the work of Bernstein (1961 and 1975), Bernstein and Henderson (1969) and Holland (1980) suggesting the existence of qualitatively distinct modes of socialization in old and new middle class homes, helped further clarify an agenda for enquiry. According to these analyses, socialization in many new middle class households takes place via relatively open forms of intergenerational communication, an implicit system of rules, and a system of social control organized around linguistically elaborated meanings. Patterns of socialization within *person-oriented* families such as these (Bernstein, 1971) may therefore be instrumental in ensuring the development of qualitatively different orientations towards formal education among their members from those in the more positional family types characteristic of the working and old middle classes.

Additionally, it was felt that an ethnographic investigation of new middle class homes might hold the potential to identify the specificity of the weak forms of classification and framing which Bernstein (1975) has also claimed to characterize the homes of those concerned with the dissemination and reproduction of forms of symbolic control. In particular, he has argued that the households of agents of symbolic control can be distinguished from others in terms of their spatial and temporal ordering such that there is, '. . . a celebration of the present over the past, the subjective over the objective, the personal over the positional . . .'.

Bernstein has further identified in such homes both a weakening in the classification of domestic categories and practices, and a strengthening of the autonomy of those socialized within them to negotiate occasions on which to become involved in personally developmental practice.

Finally, it was expected that within such settings there might be evidence suggesting a blurring of distinctions between work and leisure — between paid employment and personal enjoyment. Parental involvement in *symbolically narcissistic* forms of practice — ones which simultaneously allow for personal satisfaction and outward prestige, was similarly anticipated (Bernstein, 1975). However, once again the specificity of these, and their consequences for those concerned, remained relatively open issues for empirical enquiry.

In carrying out fieldwork in respondents' homes I was aware of the danger of assuming that male and female students would share similar experiences, since as MacDonald/Arnot's (1981a) work has shown, associated with a particular class location will be specific forms of gender socialization.

In consequence, fieldwork in students' homes set out to provide an analysis of patterns of domestic organization, as well as of the consequences of these for those experiencing them. As anticipated, subsequent field experience helped refine my overall understanding of some of the patterns of practice earlier identified. It also provided evidence for the existence of a. somewhat different set of critical dimensions to students' home experience from some of those anticipated. In particular, it enabled the identification of previously undocumented patterns of practice relating to the admission of specific categories of outsider to the home, the apportionment and use of domestic space, the establishment of specific criteria denoting degrees of cultural 'acceptability' and 'non-acceptability', and to the encouragement of student involvement in distinctive forms of intimate and sexual relationship.

Public and Private Spheres of Experience

Fieldwork in students' homes enabled the identification of a number of processes ensuring that the socialization of their residents was of a distinctive kind. Four of these strategies involved a selective importing into the household of specific categories of person or forms of experience.

The first involved the taking in of lodgers and guests. Many households rented out rooms to students from local institutions of higher education or, alternatively, offered accommodation to specific groups of individuals perceived to be in some way 'in need' of this. A second strategy was that whereby certain friends and acquaintances of the household unit were encouraged to 'drop in' on the home 'when passing'. A third related to the use of the home as a base for neighbourhood 'self-help' groups of a formal or informal kind. Finally, the apportionment and use of physical space within homes was such that within each, areas existed for the public display of artefacts associated with the cultural interests and commitments of household members. Each of these strategies was organized, at the level of intention, around ideologies of care and a public display of caring for the self, for cultural similars and selected others, or for the neighbourhood and community.

The Taking In of Lodgers and Guests as Friends of the Household

Fifteen of the households visited regularly rented out rooms. Tenants for these, however, were not obtained via advertisements in the local press but from the accommodation lists of local institutions of higher education or by word of mouth. In consequence, the majority of lodgers were students, teachers or friends who were temporarily without accommodation. In a number of cases, the renting out of rooms had commenced immediately after marital breakups in order to create an additional source of household income. Both Jill Francis' and Nigel Stewart's mothers, for example, had started taking paying guests after separating from their spouses. At the time of the fieldwork, the top floor of the Francis household was occupied by two such tenants of long standing:

> ... Who are Penny and Bill? Do they own the house as well? (PA)
> ... Well, we own the house. Bill is a painter and Penny is a teacher and they have two small children. Mum took them in when we moved here just after she and Dad split up so that they could help pay for the house ... (*Jill*, Interview, September 1981)

In a similar way, Nigel recalled the lodgers who had been taken in once his father had left home:

> ... And then we used to have all these students. Every time we didn't have enough money, we (Nigel and his brother) had to go into one bedroom so that Mum could get more lodgers in ...
> ... Where did they come from? (PA) ...
> ... The University, language schools, the 'Royal School of Languages', people she knew through someone else ... (*Nigel*, Interview, December 1981)

There was, however, another kind of guest likely to be resident in the households concerned. These were people perceived as being in special need of support and 'care'. Nigel Stewart, Jill Francis, Dave Lane, Barbara Blare, Brenda Miller and Wanda Wilson all recalled lodgers of this type having been offered accommodation from time to time:

> ... And we used to have different people staying there — people from broken homes. If they had been in trouble, they used to stay at our house ...

> ... Why was that? (PA) ...
>
> ... Because my mother decided she would rather have people
> who were in trouble, or who were in a state, come to the
> house and stay at the house than have us go out on the street
> and be with them ...
>
> ... In the house? Where did she get them from? (PA) ...
>
> ... They were friends of my brother, most of them. Because
> my brother used to go around with troublemakers and things.
> And she would bring them in because they would be having
> trouble at home at that age ... (*Barbara*, Interview, January
> 1982)

Similarly, there were occasions on which Brenda's father looked
after Stuart Jones, an art student who tended to arrive at the house late
at night with little warning, few belongings, no money, hungry and
generally the worse for wear. Wanda's mother too, offered temporary
accommodation to local students and rented out rooms to friends of
members of her household when domestic and emotional crises affecting them necessitated it. Additionally, guests of a rather different kind
were invited to stay in the Wilson home from time to time. For
example, Max, a music lecturer at the local university, was invited
to stay for some months after he had attempted suicide following
a break-up with his boyfriend. When asked why such an offer of
accommodation had been made, Wanda's mother replied,

> ... Well, it's better to have him here than for me to have to go
> to see him and hold his hand in hospital in the middle of the
> night ... (*Mrs Wilson*, Fieldnotes, February 1981)

The view that it was better to have individuals experiencing
emotional difficulty safely within the home, rather than outside it,
was one operated with by the majority of households in this study. At
first sight, the use of such a strategy would seem to imply a certain
benevolence on the part of those involved. However, rather less
positively such actions may also be viewed as efforts to intensify the
surveillance exerted by parents over their children and those with
whom they came into contact. In such ways, household members and
their friends came to be subjected to processes of invisible screening,
as parents monitored the course and nature of their personal and social
development.

A further feature of some significance concerned the manner in
which the suitability of individuals to be invited into the home came
to be assessed. While initial observations had suggested that the wel-

coming of outsiders into the home displayed a marked openness, it subsequently became apparent that the majority of those so admitted shared certain features in common, being either students from local institutions of higher education, teachers or artists. One effect of the extension of this type of household custodianship and care was therefore to selectively blur aspects of public and private worlds of experience. Incorporated into the home in consequence were a particular set of categories of experience associated with academic study, the dramatic and fine arts, and formal pedagogic practice.

The Encouragement of 'Dropping In'

In seven of the homes visited, the front doors were left unlocked throughout the day and evening. In the remainder, it was common practice to leave either the back or side entrance in a similar state. In consequence, these homes were environments through which there was a near constant flow of visitors. As Stuart commented,

> ... There were always people coming in and out of the house. We always had the backdoor open. We never locked it. We had nothing really valuable so people just dropped in and out all the time. It was just like Paddington station really ... (*Stuart*, Interview, December 1981)

When parents were asked whether they objected to these patterns of visiting, their responses showed some ambivalence. Jill's mother, for example, said:

> ... I don't mind them really. After all, it shows that Robin and Jill have friends. But I do object to sometimes coming back late at night to find the kitchen full of young boys, none of whom I know ... (*Mrs Francis*, Fieldnotes, May 1981)

Tensions like these, between pride and concern, meant that on many evenings, parents would stay up late at night when friends of their daughters and sons 'dropped in'. In such ways, they were able to maintain some influence over the social activities of their own children and those with whom the latter came into contact.

Occasionally, parents would intervene to stop these processes of visiting for a few days. At one point, for example, Tim and Elaine Scotwell's mother decided to restrict the access of Tim's friends to her home. She started by locking the front door in the evening. When she found that this had little effect, she changed the front and back door locks to ensure that she would have some say over who was to be allowed access to the home late at night. However, her attempts to intervene in this way were far from consistently applied and within ten days Tim once more had a full set of house keys in his possession and previous patterns of activity were quickly re-established.

Parents often discussed with one another the nature of students' current activities and relationships. One effect of this was to enable processes of social comparison to take place by which different sets of parents were able to display their relative degrees of insight into the activities of their own children and those of others. In such ways, status differences came to be established between different heads of household, with the highest prestige being claimed by parents such as Mrs Scotwell who appeared to know most about students' private lives. She, for example, held regular 'audiences' on Monday mornings for other parents, during which she would regale them with details of activities and exploits over the weekend. Parents such as her were also used by other heads of household as relatively reliable sources of information on their own daughters' and sons' social involvements.

Processes such as these had a number of distinctive consequences for heads of the households studied. First, they made available to parents, albeit in a commodified form, knowledge about students' social activities away from home. Second, they allowed an extension of invisible screening to sites which were not directly open to parental surveillance. Third, and of critical significance to parents in their attempts to encourage highly *personalizing* forms of socialization, these processes provided access to many of the meanings motivating the social practices preferred by students. These could subsequently be subjected to more insistent forms of interrogation than might otherwise have been the case. As Mr Cooper remarked,

> ... Of course I would never dream of suggesting that Ric was mixing with the wrong sort of people when they are here. But when they're not, if I've actually been there watching what goes on, I know more of what I'm talking about when it comes to arguing that he shouldn't spend so much of his time with them ... (*Mr Cooper*, Fieldnotes, February 1981)

The Establishment of Community Self-help Groups

The third way in which households were able to establish a distinctive quality to the type of socialization they provided for their members

was through the organization of both formal and informal neighbourhood self-help groups that used the home as a base.

The Miller household, for example, lived in a quiet residential
street in Spatown, close to three others involved in the study: the
Williams, the Coopers and the Stewarts. In everyday conversation
with one another, members of these households made frequent reference to 'The Street', likening the intimacy of their relationships with
one another to those of characters in 'Coronation Street'. Frequent
reference was also made to the fact that these households provided
physical and social support for one another in times of sickness or
trouble. The heads of household concerned would visit one another
throughout the day and evening, exchanging significant services as the
need arose. For example, when Brenda Miller's father was taken
seriously ill for some weeks, Mrs Cooper provided help to the household by helping with the shopping, preparation of food and washing.
Similarly, some years previously, Mr and Mrs Miller had provided
weekend support to members of the Cooper household when Mr and
Mrs Cooper had found it necessary to make visits abroad in search of
exotic new toys for their children's shop.

In contrast to these relatively informal self-help groups were
those of a more official kind. Typical of such activity were the
meetings of Spatown Campaign for Nuclear Disarmament (CND)
held in Mrs Scotwell's home.

> ... (talking about Spatown CND) ... the sort of thing about
> it is that you feel you're really doing something worthwhile by
> being there. Sort of becoming a better person at the same time
> as you are helping others ... (*Mrs Scotwell*, Fieldnotes, June
> 1982)

Similarly, Mrs Burton organized meetings of Spatown Women's
Aid in her house, and Mr and Mrs Wiley organized ward meetings of
the local branch of the Labour Party, as well as sessions for a voluntary agency training marriage guidance counsellors in their home.
Meetings and rehearsals in connection with the work of local amateur
dramatic and operatic groups were seen in almost every household
visited during the course of the fieldwork.

> ... Why are you a member of the drama club? ...
> ... Well it gives me something to do in the evening. I've
> made a lot of friends that way and kept up with other people
> that I know. And we do these really interesting plays —
> Cocteau, Anouilh, things like that. Interesting plays — the

sort of thing you'd never get a chance to experience otherwise
... (*Mr Miller*, Fieldnotes, September 1981)

All of these arrangements, whether formal or informal, had similar effects for students in that they encouraged the latter to participate
in a mode of socialization where there were clear-cut connections
between individually developmental forms of practice and an *overt
display of personal commitment* to a limited range of cultural options.
Furthermore, they helped provide respondents from an early age with
specific modes of cultural acquaintanceship, ones which I shall argue
are of fundamental importance in mediating students' later evaluation
of different spheres of social practice.

A final set of practices relating to the use of the home as an arena
for self and community help concerned the way in which those heads
of household who were teachers in further or higher education used
their houses as bases for tutorial and seminar work. Mrs Burton, for
example, held weekly 'academic soirées' for her Polytechnic students
in her home. Mr Deutsch similarly organized summer play readings for
his students in the garden and Mrs Miller carried out a substantial
amount of educational counselling in the kitchen. For those socialized
within such homes, there would therefore seem to exist less clear-cut
distinctions between contexts and occasions associated with paid employment and those associated with leisure. As I shall later argue,
modes of practice such as these were to have consequences for the
types of employment which students themselves later sought, since
these too tended to be those where there existed some weakening of
distinctions between work and non-work.

The Apportionment and Use of Space Within the Home

Processes such as those described above are likely to create demands
for domestic space quite different from those associated with more
privatized forms of living. To some extent, these demands were
accommodated by the physically large size of the houses themselves.
However, within their spatial ordering there existed other dimensions
of some significance for those socialized within them.

In ten homes there was a large open-plan kitchen/living area in
which a considerable amount of time would be spent by members of
the household and those visiting them. In each case, there was a large
scrubbed wooden table in the centre of the room surrounded by an
assortment of striped or brightly painted wooden chairs. The walls of

these kitchen/living areas were frequently decorated with postcards, children's paintings and drawings and posters advertising fine art exhibitions or contemporary dance. Magazines and books would lie stacked on shelves or would spill out of cupboards. Objects purchased that day, be they edible or otherwise, would often be left half-unwrapped and available for view, either on table-tops or on working-surfaces. At first sight such settings gave the impression that almost any object might have found itself at home in such a context, as toilet rolls, half-eaten apple pies, aerosol deodorants, recent airmail letters and copies of Shakespeare's plays lay jumbled together. However, it soon became clear that the majority of objects visible occupied, and helped define, certain cultural parameters, identifying what I shall describe as *culturally acceptable* forms of experience.

Clues pointing to the nature of this category were first obtained from the nature of those artefacts which were most insistently display-ed in such settings. Hence, postcards depicting scenes overseas were more conspicuous in their presentation than were those of British holiday resorts. Similarly, posters advertising fine art exhibitions in London, Paris, or Milan tended to be more prominently displayed than were those relating to work to be viewed in local art galleries. Airmail letters were left visible for longer periods of time than were those from friends at home. In all of these cases it is possible to detect an overriding concern with foreign and culturally exotic forms of practice. However, this was compounded by a concurrent interest in objects which were individually rather than mass produced. Hence, artefacts of collage, craft and clay were more visible in such settings than were bulk produced plastic articles for popular consumption. Examples of children's or young people's art, especially if produced by those resident in the home, were given particular prominence, conveying an *authenticity* lacking in that of more adult household members.

In an effort to explore students' own perceptions of these dis-plays, I asked on many occasions what it would be unthinkable to have within the home. Most had difficulty in replying, but when prompted felt that objection would be most likely to be made to ready-made, everyday articles produced for popular consumption.

> ... Would there be any objects you couldn't bring into the house? (PA)
> ... Objects? What do you mean? Things that are not tasteful? Oh, I don't know. I take things back which I find in the street. Like those big plastic things that you find around roadworks.

And I leave them under the table until I can think what I'm going to do with them. And then I find that I'm not going to do anything with them and so I chuck them out. No, I don't think there's anything I couldn't bring back if I wanted to. No, we don't pick and choose I can tell you! ...

... No, I was wondering if there were any objects which it would be unthinkable to bring in (PA) ...

... Well, I think that if I brought in one of those cheap paper lampshades which students seem to have, my mother would say ... she'd wonder about it ...

... What do you mean? Those paper ones? (PA) ...

... Yes, she'd wonder why. But she'd put up with it. There's nothing was couldn't really bring in ... (*Jill*, Interview, September 1981)

From the above description, it is possible to see that even mass-produced objects such as items of street furniture could be imbued with a certain authenticity once effort had been made to transform them into works of 'art'. Nevertheless, as the above data shows, for students and their parents there clearly existed a category of social experience to be 'wondered about': one more mundane than those that are either exotic or intrinsically authentic.

A description of two other homes will help clarify certain of the evaluative dimensions which the preceding analysis has pointed to. Dave Lane also lived in a house with such an open-plan kitchen/living area, this time on its lower ground floor. The walls of this room had been white-washed by his mother using natural materials she had brought back from a recent trip to France, and a wood burning stove had been installed to combat the chill which seeped up from the 200-year-old stone-flagged floor. The major items of furniture in this living area were a scrubbed oak table and an array of second-hand wall cupboards without doors to them. On the shelves of these cupboards were prominently displayed a number of clear glass jars containing varieties of pasta, rice, lentils and other dried foods. Posters were very much in evidence both within this room and elsewhere. Many of them advertised exhibitions of the work of artists who were friends of the household. Additionally, the front windows of the house displayed stickers proclaiming Dave's mother's identification with ecological concerns, animal rights, the women's movement and opposition to nuclear energy, Visitors were to be found at all times of the day and night sitting around the table in the kitchen/living area, talking about films, books and theatre, drinking Earl Grey tea and sharing gossip about others who they knew.

The communal living area in Ric Cooper's house similarly occupied a basement and took the form of a modernized Victorian kitchen. It had a recently relaid stone floor, an Aga cooker in the place of the old kitchen range and scrubbed wooden work surfaces around its walls. On top of these were an immense variety of brown earthenware pots, wooden kitchen implements and cast iron pans. Such a display of culinary authenticity was offset by the juxtaposition of two modern food processors and expensive split-level cooking facilities of Scandinavian origin.

It is therefore possible to see how households in this study were intentionally ordered so as not only to affirm an acquaintanceship with temporally and geographically exotic forms of practice, but also so as to bear witness to the personal and political commitments of their adult members. The existence of *cultural affirmations* such as these was to have consequences for students themselves many of whom made effective comparisons between the organization of domestic space in their own homes and that in others they had visited:

> ... I remember when I had to go and live in this friend's house for a while just after Dad died ... in this very modest housing estate where everyone was into keeping up with their neighbours. The housewives there used to dust their back lawns! I stayed with these people, and they had just had an extension built ... and she had a part-time job, painted nails and dressed very smartly. And he worked in town from nine to five. They were so normal. They had a freezer and a tumble drier, and they used to cook this frozen food for tea — fish fingers and peas and chips! Ugh! And their sitting room ... they had it all done out! They were so proud of their sitting room — carpet, table, sideboard, corner-unit and colour tv. And they had one ornament on the mantle-piece and that was it! Ugh! ... (*Susan*, Interview, December 1981)

Evidence for the operation of principles of inclusion and exclusion affecting the apportionment and use of domestic space was to be found not only in the kitchen and living areas of the homes visited. Ground floor toilets and bathrooms were similarly organized, with postcard, poster and sticker displays also decorating their walls. These particular modes of practice effected not only an affirmation of the personal and political commitments of household members, but also encouraged acquaintanceship with specific types of cultural experience for those whose socialization they mediated. A selective blurring of distinctions between public and private spheres of practice thereby took place with rather special consequences for those who experienced it.

Affirmation and the Intentioned Provision of Culturally Acceptable Experience

The parameters identifying culturally acceptable experience within students' homes were further consolidated by a set of cultural affirmations through which parents ensured that students gained certain 'worthwhile' experiences. A clear majority of parents had encouraged their daughters and sons to travel widely. As Nigel commented,

> ... Mum used to work overtime so that she could take us to Yugoslavia, because she believed in us travelling. If she could ever get money, she would send us abroad, holidays from school and so on ...
> ... Why did she believe in that? (PA)
> ... Because she thought it was educational. More educational than school. It was a valuable thing to do. She sent us off to Austria and then she went to Yugoslavia and we went to Venice with her ... (*Nigel*, Interview, December 1981)

Similarly, when I interviewed Jill just after she had returned from a holiday in Florence, it became clear that she too had been subject to parental pressure to extend her experience of the world.

> ... You've been in Italy recently. What have you been doing there? (PA)
> ... Seeing all those paintings that I learned about in art history. Just travelling around visiting places, swimming, you know, Rome, Paris, Milan, Naples, Florence. ... We knew someone who owns a flat in Rome through my mother and we stayed there for a week ...
> ... What are you thinking of doing over the next few weeks?
> ... I keep avoiding the situation, the subject, really. People keep asking me and I just don't know. I might go and live in France. And also I met this woman who runs a restaurant in Switzerland and she employs foreign waitresses so I might just go out there. Mum wants me to go away anyway to get

some more experience of the world ... (*Jill*, Interview, September 1981)

Carol too had travelled extensively in America and Italy.

... Well I went to America, sort of at the end of the summer, for about three months and came back and then had a lot of problems with this bloke I was living with ... and then I got really depressed when I came back. And then my father said he would pay for me to and study Italian for three months. So I went to Florence and I stayed on a bit afterwards and travelled a bit ... (*Carol*, Interview, May 1981)

Without exception, every student had travelled widely in Europe, some in North America as well. However, travel abroad took a specific form. It was always independently organized, never through a travel company, and often involved travelling or hitching with a friend. Furthermore, not once did I hear overseas travel talked about in terms of the opportunity for relaxation it might afford. Rather, it was undertaken in order to view works of art, meet new and 'interesting' people, see exotic and far-off places and to 'broaden' cultural horizons.

Interestingly enough, on occasions when residence in Spatown meant that students were unable to directly experience the cultural exoticism of far-off locations, vicarious provision was made for this by their parents who interspersed their descriptions of events with foreign phrases. So, food would be taken 'al fresco' in the summer, Perrier water on ice would be 'de rigueur' after a shopping expedition and fixtures and fittings picked up in Saturday morning antiques markets would be endearingly referred to as 'objets trouvés'.

Another strategy to ensure the consolidation of students' acquaintance with *culturally acceptable* experience involved the 'staging' of political discussions and arguments at mealtimes. Parents would use such opportunities to express their own political views about issues of the day and to solicit the opinions of others present. On one such occasion, Brenda's mother sat down at the kitchen table with the following comment,

... Well, I think Thatcher and Reagan are mad. They won't be happy until they've destroyed the whole world together. I think I'm going to the CND march this weekend. Who's coming with me? ... (*Mrs Miller*, Fieldnotes, October 1981)

On another occasion, Tim and Elaine's mother remarked,

> ... Elaine and I went on the anti-abortion rally the other
> weekend. It was so good. There were so many people from
> Spatown that they had to lay on extra coaches as well as the
> train ...
> ... Yes, Mum thought it was just like the good old days on
> CND marches in the fifties!
> ... You may well laugh, but someone's got to do something
> about these things. Otherwise that Bill will get through and
> then what about a woman's right to choose? ... (*Mrs Scotwell
> and Elaine*, Fieldnotes, October 1980)

Parents' efforts to make their political opinions known to others
were not un-noticed by students themselves.

> ... The thing about Sarah's (a student from Spatown College
> who was not included in the sample) Mum that makes her
> different from mine is that her Mum is a 'Mum' in public and
> is political privately, whereas my Mum is political in public
> and is only sometimes a 'Mum' to me at home ... (*Brenda*,
> Fieldnotes, April 1982)

A further series of cultural affirmations within the home related
to the ways in which time away from parental surveillance, the use of
drugs and the gaining of sexual experience came to be negotiated.
From an early age, students had been encouraged to stay out late at
night and to make their own decisions about who they spent their
time with, when they ate and so on. However, this autonomy was
only allowed if prior negotiation had taken place between them and
their parents. Such negotiations required respondents to elaborate
upon their intentions and were sometimes followed by parents emphasizing the importance of 'being sensible' and 'being responsible'.

> ... I've always been able to go out when I wanted to and do
> what I liked, and my parents never stopped me. But like, all
> the people at school, their parents used to say that they had to
> be in by 10.00 and things like that ...
> ... So your parents never used to restrict you? (PA)
> ... No. They never used to say anything except ask me where
> I was off to. In fact, for a time I thought they didn't love me
> bacause all the other kids I knew, their parents used to say they
> had to be in by such and such a time. And I thought that my
> ones didn't really care because they never stopped me from
> going anywhere. And afterwards I realized that they sort of
> trusted me ... (*Barbara*, Interview, October 1981)

... As long as I can remember, I've been able to do what I want, go where I want, be with who I want in the evening. No, mum and dad never restricted me. I had to explain where I was going and all that, but they would always let me do what I wanted to. No problem there. (*Jim*, Interview, February 1982)

However, as fieldwork subsequently showed, there were differential limits to this liberalism for female and male students. The former were more insistently questioned about what they intended doing when they went out than were the latter. In particular, within this context parents seemed particularly keen to explore the nature of their daughters' potential heterosexual relationships. As Jane explains,

... The only restrictions were that I used to have to tell my parents where I was. That was the only thing they used to worry about. My mother was terribly upset about me sleeping with anybody without telling her first. ... But apart from that, I did have quite a free upbringing ... (*Jane*, Interview, September 1981)

For the majority of female students, negotiating absence from the home often required them to be relatively explicit about their sexual intentions, the seriousness of their proposed involvements and the forms of contraception they were likely to use. Males on the other hand were more readily granted permission, and even encouraged, to either absent themselves overnight for the purposes of heterosexual liaisons or to have their partners stay overnight at home.

... I can remember when I started bringing girls back ... No one said anything but I got the feeling that they were really rather proud ... (*Phil*, Interview, January 1982)

... One of the things I really regret now is that mum didn't restrain me from bringing back different girls at night. In view of all the trouble that caused in later relationships, I wish she had done so ... (*Dave*, Fieldnotes, May 1982)

Such was the effect of these rather different strategies by which parents encouraged female and male students in their heterosexual activity, that for some females at least, asking a male to stay overnight was out of the question unless parents had been previously informed.

... It would be unthinkable for me to have a boyfriend to stay overnight without mum having met him first of all. It would just upset her too much ... (*Norma*, Interview, June 1981)

Within many homes, parents' attitudes towards the use of alcohol and 'soft' drugs seemed at first sight similarly liberal. Students had been encouraged from an early age to drink alcohol with meals and at parties.

> ... Well, first I had wine with water. I suppose that was when I was 7 or 8. Then I used to get a glass to myself. Then there would be cider whenever mum had one of her parties. It's just that it's always been there ... funny really ... (*Ric*, Interview, November 1981)

Similarly, a number of respondents' first introduction to marijuana had been through their parents, many of whom believed that smoking tobacco was infinitely more dangerous than smoking marijuana.

> ... I don't know ... I smoked my first joint when I was about 8 years old ... with my parents ... I mean, I could do things which they agreed with really, things which they thought were all right. I suppose we were just very open in our family ... (*Jane*, Interview, September 1981)

> ... Oh, we're not allowed to smoke cigarettes at home. But Robin can smoke dope, but Mum won't let him smoke cigarettes ... because she's worried about his health ... (*Jill*, Interview, September 1981)

When I asked parents about their attitudes to students' use of alcohol and drugs, for the large part their responses suggested that provided such activities were carried out under surveillance within the home, little harm could come of them. Only if they took place unsupervised might trouble ensue.

> ... Well, I think it's better for them to do it here than for them to be introduced to it by some pusher at a party miles away. Anyway, I don't want them to think that there's anything special about it ... (*Mr Deutsch*, Fieldnotes, July 1981)

Paradoxically, however, parents' efforts to supervise and control the use of alcohol and drugs had somewhat contradictory effects, since they encouraged students to seek opportunities away from home when they wanted to use alcohol or drugs such as marijuana in ways that might have been disapproved of by parents. Respondents identified numerous occasions when they had made some excuse to their parents about 'meeting a friend' or 'going to the cinema' when, in reality, their intention had been to get drunk, wrecked or stoned. Parents' efforts to regulate the use of alcohol and 'soft' drugs thereby not only ensured students' familiarity with these substances but encouraged the acquisition of two rather different styles of use — one within the home, the other outside of it.

Cultural Affirmation and Sexuality

Students' homes could also be distinguished in terms of the openness with which sex was discussed within them. Indeed, a great deal of time and energy was invested in talking about sex in general, the sexual behaviour of others and what 'good' sex should be about. Visitors would frequently be embroiled in such discussions within minutes of their arrival. Only rarely however, were personal experiences referred to. Thus, while Tom's mother made frequent reference to her work as a 'registered sex counsellor', a 'sex therapist' and a 'marriage guidance expert', she rarely talked about her own sexual experiences. On the other hand, discussions about sex frequently centred around the importance of industrious, diligent and committed heterosexual activity, with parents arguing that heterosexual relationships in particular were something that had to be 'worked hard at' to make them satisfying.

> ... But surely it's natural to have sex? (PA)
> ... Don't you believe it. It's something that has to be worked at, read about, thought about. You see that time and time again in my marriage guidance work ... (*Mrs Miller*, Fieldnotes, April 1982)

Students' homes contained numerous manuals and guides to good heterosexual technique. Books such as Alex Comfort's *The Joy of Sex*, were often found lying casually on coffee tables or amonst magazines piled up in bathrooms. Students' parents considered that they regulated their own sexual relationships with precision and thoroughness. Jim's mother recounted how her former husband has,

> ... never been satisfied until I had had at least one orgasm. There I would be, trying like mad with him working away. In the end, I just gave up pretending ... (*Mrs Grant*, Fieldnotes, September 1981)

In a similarly 'scientific' and industrious manner, parents took sexual partners other than those with whom they shared long-term relationships. Weekends were often occasions for parties during which it was not unusual for parents to pair off with one another. Many an affair between them started this way. Such practices were not uncommented upon by students.

> ... And do all the parents know each other? (PA)
> ... Yes, it's really odd because they do ... and they socialize very easily. And all the parents seem to have affairs with one another which is really funny. ... Like Mary Wilson's mother is having an affair with someone else. Brian Simpson's mother's having an affair with Rupert Green and father of Jillie. Oh and the Welch lot are always at it ... (*Jill*, Interview, November 1981)

In the days following such parties, extensive discussion would take place about the quality of the various sexual liaisons that had taken place, but within these too there was once again a striking absence of personal reference. This tendency to analyze the quality of sexual experience in terms of the diligence and industry of those involved testifies to the invasion of this sphere of practice by an ethic of achievement (Wolfenstein, 1951; Cohen and Taylor, 1976). Seen this way, 'Orgasm, which is a "form of work", is a deadly serious affair with strict standards of correct behaviour' (Heath, 1982). Heterosexual relationships for students' parents had to be seen to be diligently worked at, otherwise they lacked both authenticity and the capacity to be personally fulfilling.

Paralleling discursive structures such as these were those which affirmed household acquaintance with the sexual involvements of openly gay men within Spatown's artistic community. Few households were unfamiliar with Max, a lecturer in music at the local university. Wanda Wilson's family regularly provided overnight accommodation for him during personal crises, but he was also a close personal friend of Jill, Susan and Dave's mothers. Paul Sullivan, a former youth worker at Spatown's Youth Centre and a keen director of amateur opera productions, was similarly well known to parents. He too was regularly offered overnight accommodation within a number of households. Both of these individuals were extensively talked about within students' homes. Positive and supporting references were not only made to their recent work within the local community arts scene but about those with whom they were presently sexually involved. Indeed, there was some status to be gained by being the first to know about the current status of these and other openly gay men's personal lives. It would seem, therefore, that acquaintance with the homosexual and heterosexual practices of others assumed critical significance within students' homes.

In contradiction to parents' apparent liberalism with respect to the discussion of varieties of sexual practice were the efforts they made to normalize students' own sexual involvements. By regularly questioning their daughters about their present and future heterosexual relationships, parents attempted to ensure that the latter pursued their heterosexual involvements with appropriate levels of industry and commitment. For sons, interventions were restricted (but were none the less insistent) to the case of suspected homosexual proclivities. An example of such concern could be seen in Mrs Scotwell's alarm when she suspected that her son Tim might be gay.

> ... He doesn't seem to have any girlfriends. Everyone he goes around with is male. I can't understand it. We've got to try and find out. It isn't natural ... (*Mrs Scotwell*, Fieldnotes, September 1980)

Subsequently, Tim was persuaded to seek counselling for his attributed 'problem'. Another instance of such concern can be seen in some of Dave's comments when I asked him about his mother's attitude to him spending time with Max.

> ... I can remember when I used to go round to see Max. He used to take me out for tea sometimes and Mum would always be very suspicious when she came round to pick me up. She would always give him a funny look. She never said anything, but I could see that she wasn't very happy about me being alone with him because he was gay and that ... (*Dave*, Interview, July 1982)

It is important to recognize, however, that parents were only partially successful in their attempts to influence students' sexual behaviour. In particular, efforts to ensure that sexual relationships were pursued with appropriate levels of industry and commitment had the rather contradictory effect of ensuring that relationships which did not conform to this pattern took place outside of parental surveillance away from home. Similarly, whilst male homosexual activity was not common amongst respondents, this too took place when it happened in contexts relatively safe from parental scrutiny.

Conclusions

At the beginning of this chapter I suggested (following Bernstein, 1975) that new middle class households such as those investigated in this study might be characterized by the existence of weak classificatory relationships within them. Furthermore, it was also anticipated that relations within these households would be relatively weakly framed, allowing those within them considerable autonomy with respect to decision making. Both of these predictions would seem to be borne out by the evidence presented above.

Three interrelated classificatory relationships in particular would seem to have been weakened in students' homes. First, there was a weakening of the distinction between adult and child practices. Evidence for this is provided by parents' attempts to introduce students at an early age to alcohol, marijuana and specific discourses about sexual practice.

Second, there was a blurring of the distinction between work and leisure. Many of the activities which parents involved themselves in within the home were clearly work-related. Many of their leisure pursuits such as involvement in the theatre and community arts were extensions of the sorts of activity they undertook in their paid employment outside the home.

Third, the taking-in of lodgers and guests and the setting up of self-help community groups all bear witness to a weakening of the distinction between clearly identifiable public and private realms of experience. Parents' efforts to ensure students' familiarity with theatre, ballet and fine art (elements of culture which within many households have a 'distant' 'out there' quality to them) provide yet further evidence of the weakening of this major classificatory relationship. Somewhat paradoxically, however, the specificity of the persons, objects and events that were thereby encouraged to enter the home helped establish a strong classificatory relationship between *culturally acceptable* and *culturally non-acceptable* spheres of practice.

The insulation between categories created by this classificatory relationship is of interest for two reasons. Firstly, its existence suppresses the arbitrariness of the cultural distinctions it creates, making these seem 'natural' and 'inevitable' to those who experience them (Bernstein, 1982). *Cultural acceptability* comes thereby to be seen, not as a social evaluation but as something which inheres in people, objects and practices themselves. Secondly, it is of significance because daily experience of this insulation gives rise to categories of agents who can recognize and reproduce the 'legitimate' cultural domain which it identifies (Bourdieu, 1971). As will be seen in the following chapter, this ability to discriminate between two differentially evaluated cultural spheres was to have profound consequences for students' negotiation of formal educational contexts.

Because students were allowed considerable personal autonomy with respect to what they did within the home and when they were absent from it, there was also considerable evidence of a weak framing of social relations within the households visited.

Socialization through the *invisible pedagogy* (Bernstein, 1975) created by the weak classificatory relationships and weak frames described, had both intended and unintended consequences for students. At the first of these levels, it encouraged the acquisition of certain perceptual and evaluative competences by which they could respond to events around them. It also helped students develop skills by which to challenge the expectations and demands of others around them. Many of these skills involved the use of elaborated forms of verbal communication in processes of personal disavowal. For an analysis of the unintended consequences of this particular type of socialization we must explore what happens when competences such as these are transported from the home to other sites of experience.

Chapter 4

School and College

Introduction

In the previous chapter it was suggested that weakly classified aspects of students' home life created distinctions between *culturally acceptable* and *culturally non-acceptable* spheres of practice. It was further argued that criteria connoting cultural acceptability within such settings could be distinguished in terms of foreignness, exoticness and the everyday-once-transformed. Finally, it was suggested that dominant modes of socialization within students' homes could be characterized by their concern to allow those socialized within them considerable autonomy with respect to the negotiation of social situations.

In this chapter, efforts will be made to examine the relationship between students' home experience and that gained in formal educational contexts. I shall also look at the effects of such articulations for the creation of yet further distinctions significant to respondents and their parents. While respondents displayed synchronic homogeneity by their presence on GCE Advanced level courses at Spatown College in 1979, it is important to recognize that they had achieved this common status by a number of different routes. Nevertheless, while students differed from one another in terms of the detail of their primary and secondary education, there were similarities between them in terms of the broad types of educational experience they had gained prior to College, their reactions to this and the role their parents had played in securing it.

There are a number of studies which detail the reasons why many 16–18 year-old students in Britain prefer to attend colleges of further education for GCE study rather than the sixth-forms of schools (Trustram, 1967; Cook, 1970; Young, 1971; Schools Council, 1970). Many of these investigations suggest that students' efforts to reject the restrictions that schools impose on their personal freedom are an important precipitating factor underlying such transitions. Additionally, Moore (1972) and Rattigan (1978) have identified a concern among some young people undertaking GCE study to *actively seek* locations where personal autonomy is encouraged. We might therefore reasonably conclude that for many young people, the transition from school to college at 16 is motivated by both push and pull factors. In this chapter, therefore, I will describe how students negotiated their educational experience before arriving at Spatown College. Efforts will be made to identify both positive and negative responses on the part of students to secondary school experience. I shall also explore the way in which home experience as well as parental support and encouragement contributed to the educational trajectories in this study.

Educational Trajectories

While respondents had attended a variety of schools throughout their years of formal education, it was possible to detect some common features within the nature of this educational experience. Of particular note in this respect were parental interventions to ensure that students' educational experience would be of a certain type. At the primary school level, such parental interventions usually focussed around the securing of 'open' or 'free' forms of educational experience.

Fourteen students had attended primary schools selected by their parents with integrated day provision and child-centred forms of teaching. Jane described her primary school as follows:

> ... You didn't have to wear school uniform there. I learned nothing there at all ...
> ... Why was that? ...
> ... Because I think it was just sort of such a free school. I mean ... like I'm so lazy as a person, and you made these sort of blocks with each subject on them and at the end of the week you had to have all your blocks up on this container on the wall. So you used to put them there anyway without doing any work. Everyone did and it just didn't work very well ... I used to enjoy primary school ... (*Jane*, Interview, September 1981)

A further three respondents had attended fee-paying Free Schools:

> ... I used to go to Free School in Broadville ... to a Free School right? You pay fees and do what you want. The idea is

that each stage you go through, if you learn something you will learn it better because you want to ... yeah? ... (*Norma*, Interview, June 1981)

... What sort of primary school did you go to? (PA)
... It was a really experimental Free School. It was really good except that they neglected things like English and maths
...
... What sort of methods did they use? (PA)
... Well ... they left you totally to yourself. A bit like college really! I mean ... at the beginning of the week you had this book. And you had to do certain things that you had to do ... and you could do all these things when you felt like it ... (*Jill*, Interview, September 1981)

Parents' interest in securing particular types of educational experience for students was closely related to other more general concerns associated with the provision of specific modes of socialization. As Norma put it,

... At the moment she's bringing up Robert, my brother, who is 2, and she's still breast feeding him. She will probably do that until he is 5, just like she did with my sister. And since he's her last kid probably, she really wants to bring him up like she'd really like to bring a child up. And like everything that he wants to do, like he's not spoiled or anything, like if he sees a new thing and wants to get into it, there are no barriers. I think it's really funny sometimes, but it's really nice ... (*Norma*, Interview, July 1981)

Parental intervention in the educational process also took place at transfer from primary to secondary school. At the time of the study, state secondary schooling in Spatown was available in five single sex comprehensive schools and one mixed comprehensive school with limited sixth-form provision. There were, however, mixed comprehensive schools in nearby conurbations and there were also a number of single sex fee-paying schools in the city. Respondents' parents, however, felt it important that their offspring were educated in schools that were both comprehensive and coeducational. Jill's and Norma's parents, for example, had visited a large number of single sex schools in Spatown with their daughters before reaching the decision to send them to a mixed school some five miles away. Similarly, Dave's mother had arranged for him to attend a mixed comprehensive school some ten miles from Spatown. Tim and Elaine's parents moved house within Spatown to be close to the only mixed secondary school within the city boundaries. As Mrs Scotwell commented,

> ... Really there could be no question of us sending Tim or Elaine to the sort of single sex school we have in this place. It's not natural for them to spend all that time in the company of the same sex. It just makes for problems later on ... (*Mrs Scotwell*, Fieldnotes, March 1982)

There were, however, elements of tension within decisions such as these, since co-educational schools in, and near to, Spatown were perceived by parents as having less established academic reputations than did the single sex institutions (many of which had been selective grammar schools until the mid-1970s when comprehensive reorganization had taken place). Jane's mother showed a particular awareness of this.

> ... I think when we moved to Spatown we were really conscious of helping Jane to make the right choice about where she wanted to go. I thought that Spatown High would be the best place because she would be able to work there. But it was a single sex school and we didn't like the thought of that much. In the end, we agreed that she should go to John Manvers (School) ... (*Mrs Burton*, Interview, April 1982)

In the case of only two students, Brenda and Carol, had a single sex secondary school been deliberately decided upon at the age of transfer. In seven other cases, respondents had been allocated to single sex comprehensive schools as a result of there being a lack of places at the one coeducational secondary school within the two boundaries. Brenda's parents' wish that she should study GCE subjects at Advanced level, and their initial belief that these were best studied at school, had resulted in her being sent to a single sex secondary school. As she recalled,

> ... Dad wouldn't let me go to John Manvers (School) because I had to go to a school where I could get my 'A' levels, which is really silly because in the end, me and Penny (her sister) and now Roger (her brother) never took them there, but ended up at college ... (*Brenda*, Fieldnotes, April 1982)

From such comments it would appear that parents experienced some conflict between the desire that their daughters and sons should be educated coeducationally and the wish that they should succeed academically. Further evidence of this dilemma can be seen in Jane's description of what happened when her family first moved to Spatown.

> ... I can remember when we moved to Spatown from Broad-ville, Mum wanted me to go to the ... High School because she thought I'd get better teaching there and I would be able to do 'A' levels and things like that. But then she also wanted me to go to a mixed school. So we went round them and then she asked me what I thought, and of course I said I wanted to go to John Manvers (School) becauses it was like the one I'd been at before. But she was never really sure I don't think ...
> (*Jane*, Interview, September 1981)

Further parental intervention took place when students reached the age of 16. In each case this involved parents supporting and even encouraging their daughters and sons to transfer from school to college of further education for further GCE study. In the case of twenty-three out of twenty-seven respondents, the desire to make such a move was related, at least in part, to their antipathy towards specific aspects of the secondary schooling process. In particular, many objected to the structured timetabling of lessons at school, the wearing of school uniform, perceived regimentation and the operation of positional forms of control.

> ... I just couldn't stand all that lining up in neat rows, going to assembly, things like that. And then there was my sister, she'd never got on at school, so the teachers assumed I wouldn't. In the end, I left there. Mum and Dad supported me because they (the teachers) were only going to let me do 'O' levels there, whereas I could do my 'A' levels at college ...
> (*Brenda*, Interview, December 1981)

Students also identified stigmatization by their contemporaries at secondary school as a contributory factor underlying the transition from school to college.

> ... I wasn't accepted by the majority of people that were there, in much the same way that Mum wasn't. We were total outcasts. We really were. I mean they hardly ever talked to me except to ask why I did the things I did ... Well, just the things that I did which everyone thought were really strange — dyeing my hair, hennaing my hair. Actually, it was the fact

that it was henna which really mattered. I mean, I used to have endless people saying, 'What's henna?' They used to say to me, 'How do you henna your hair?' 'Why don't you use normal dye?' And they used to call me freaky Jane and that ... (*Jane*, Interview, September 1981)

Less frequently, a desire to follow particular academic courses was mentioned as a reason for the move from school to college. Whatever the combination of circumstances behind the move to Spatown College, every student had undertaken this with the support of their parents at the time. It is important to recognize, however, that this support was given for a particular type of study. When I asked respondents whether they had considered undertaking more vocationally relevant courses after leaving school, the dominant response suggested that such possibilities had never been seriously considered.

... I think we all sort of presumed (when we went to college) that we were going on to university or polytechnic or somewhere, or to some sort of higher education. We had that sort of attitude. I mean, I took it for granted that was what I was going to do. You know, I wasn't thinking about work or a job or anything like that ... (*Carol*, Interview, May 1981)

Overall, students in this study were distinct in a number of ways. Most had begun their schooling in relatively experimental or open educational contexts and had progressed through deliberately chosen coeducational comprehensive schools to reach Spatown College by the age of 16. Moreover, at key stages in their educational careers, they had received significant amounts of parental support and encouragement for the choices they had made. However, their educational choices, particularly those associated with the transition from secondary school to college of further education, had been as much facilitated by antipathy towards aspects of the schooling process as by parental support and intervention.

Affirmation and Challenge Within Education

The majority of students negotiated their secondary school experience using strategies which involved both *affirmation* and *challenge*. These general categories describe practices implying relative acceptance of or relative antipathy towards aspects of the schooling process. They do not, however, have their origins within the educational context alone since, as will be seen, some of the most rejected aspects of secondary schooling were those that differed most from students' home experiences.

Challenging the Structure of Educational Experience

Many respondents objected to aspects of secondary school routine.

> ... What were the most boring things about it? What were the worst things? (PA)
> ... Just sitting through endless lessons without knowing what was going on. The constant routine, lining up and being polite to people, and not knowing what anything's for, you know ... (*Carol*, Interview, May 1981)

> ... The worst bit was having to take it from all these people (teachers) who you knew were really illiterate. They would pretend that they knew about things but they never allowed you any freedom or creativity. You had to be where they wanted you and do what they wanted you to all the time ... (*Jim*, Interview, November 1981)

Schools were perceived as institutions which oppressively regulated how individuals spent their time. We can see Wanda's antipathy to this sort of control in comments she made about the school's reaction to her interest in theatre production.

> ... Well, I wanted to form a theatre society, and that was like trying to get blood from a stone because they had these set ideas about what people in the theatre did and ... you know ... If you want a theatre society, you have to go out of school to do it. So I went out of school to do it, and then when I started to get quite good — you know, we had a rehearsal one afternoon because the BBC were coming to film us — and I had to have this amazing fight to get the afternoon off, and the only thing I was missing was games which I never went to anyway. So, when you're continuously having to fight to get into your own career because they weren't prepared to let you have the experience of what it was like, actually in the school ... (*Wanda*, Interview, February 1981)

Many students also objected to the way in which schools attempted to regulate their personal dress and appearance.

... Like, I can remember one really awful experience that I had in a maths class. This other maths teacher came in, who wasn't my teacher, but another one. He came in and I was sitting there, and like you are supposed to wear all grey for school. And I had a grey mohair jumper on with holes in it, but it was quite warm, and a pink shirt, long earrings, a blue skirt, pink socks and bright red shoes. And this guy came in, right in the middle of maths lesson and started pulling my hair. Right back, so that my head was pulled right back, and I was choking, and he said, 'My god, look at your hair. It's disgusting.' And then he pulled my shirt out and said 'What's this?. It isn't the right colour.' And then he pushed at the holes in my jumper, and he picked on everything ... (*Jackie*, Interview, September 1981)

In efforts to challenge teachers' attempts to control their behaviour, students used strategies similar to those employed in negotiating personal freedoms within the home. These involved the use of elaborated verbal communication to argue a case different from that being put by others. On some occasions such arguments led to serious confrontation within the school.

... You know, I used to argue with the headmistress over points. OK ... the majority of the points were totally trivial. But you know, just points of school uniform. And I did that once and had a very large argument with her, and got pulled up before the deputy head and got told that I wasn't allowed to talk to the headmistress like that ... (*Patsie*, Interview, December 1981)

On other occasions, students' parents too became involved in these processes of verbal justification. Jane, for example, regularly recalled how she used to walk out of school during the day because she felt that it was,

... all so silly. Really I did. I thought school was petty. The teachers were really petty ... (*Jane*, Interview, September 1981)

On a number of occasions, Jane's mother was called to the school to justify her daughter's behaviour. As Jane continued,

... I mean ... apparently ... I was only talking to my Mum about this the other day, about two months ago, but she said that if I didn't have the parents that I did, I would have got chucked out of school ... (*Jane*, Interview, September 1981)

In such ways, we can see that challenges against aspects of the schooling were those which affirmed specific sets of social competences acquired within the home. In particular, the use of elaborated forms of interpersonal communication to justify and redefine actions running contrary to the rules and regulations of the school, can be seen as modes of challenge constituted by the transportation of home-based social practices to the educational context.

Underlying most students' decision to transfer from school to Spatown College was the belief that education in this latter context would allow them greater degrees of personal autonomy.

... I went to college because I thought that I wouldn't have to come across authority. I hated having to do things like go to assembly, being there to register, having to be in school at lunch hours, that sort of thing ... (*Tom*, Interview, September 1981)

Once at college, however, students' continuing desire to retain personal control over spatial and temporal contexts was shown by the way in which they attended classes. Some of the most frequently overheard comments by teaching staff at Spatown College concerned the irregular attendance of students. When I questioned students themselves about the reasons for this, a number of similar responses seemed forthcoming.

... When I arrived at College I thought it was going to be really free and that the courses would be interesting. How wrong could I be? I mean, some of the courses were interesting, but others were really boring so I eventually gave up going to them. But then they (teachers) started asking me where I was and that, and that made me even more determined not to go to their classes ... (*Brian*, Interview, February 1982)

Students' efforts to influence the spatial and temporal ordering of secondary school contexts were therefore mirrored by similar strategies at College contesting the near equally strong way in which interaction within the latter context was framed.

Another aspect of secondary schooling which was negatively evaluated by students was the unwillingness of teachers to treat them as *persons* or individuals with rights. Instead, many teachers had responded towards them as *pupils*, a positioned category within the context of a hierarchically organized institution.

> ... The problem with school was that the teachers there treated you as if you didn't matter. They decided that they knew what was best for you. They put you in streams and sets and things, and then they left you there. You weren't a real person in their eyes, just a kid ... (*Ric*, Interview, May 1981)

> ... the actual attitude when I told them I wanted to take 'O' levels was horrific. I was told I was stupid and incapable of taking 'O' levels or 'A' levels or anything like that. The only thing they said I could do was to retake my CSEs and get a higher grade ... (*Brenda*, Interview, February 1981)

In contrast, teachers at Spatown College were evaluated much more positively in terms of their behaviour towards those whom they taught.

> ... I can remember being really amazed at Spatown College because people opened doors for each other and that sort of thing. It came as quite a shock after school. People spoke to each other and lecturers spoke to you as an equal. That totally flabbergasted me ... (*Carol*, Interview, March 1981)

> ... So you arrived at college. What did you think about it? (PA)
> ... I liked it. I mean, it was so different to school. You were free-er. You were treated like a person rather than like somebody who didn't know what they were doing.
> ... What were the sort of differences that you noticed? (PA)
> ... The fact that you didn't have to go to lectures ... that it was more mature. It's not a choice but it's your decision. You knew that if you were going to do something it was your choice and you were not going to get a detention or something for not doing it ... (*Chris*, Interview, July 1981)

So far, I have tried to identify the ways in which students challenged specific aspects of their secondary school experience. I have argued that many of these challenges took their origins, at least in part, from disjunctions between home and school experience with respect to the degree of personal autonomy allowed by each. Weakly framed, person-oriented contexts such as those within students' homes, contrast sharply with the strongly framed and positional settings characteristic of many Spatown secondary schools. Additionally, communicative strategies which were highly valued within the home were often seen within schools as instances of troublemaking or argumentativeness. We can, therefore, best understand students' challenging of aspects of the secondary schooling process as a process of contestation in which efforts are made to challenge framing values very different from those operating within the home.

Paradoxically, such challenges provided respondents with yet further practice in the use of elaborated verbal communication as a strategy for the winning of personal autonomy. Because of this, challenges such as these may further consolidate cultural differences between groups dependent upon the use of these particular sociolinguistic strategies. Additionally, parental support for transfer from secondary school to Spatown College, itself partly motivated by ideologies to do with personal development, may further encourage respondents to follow educational trajectories different from those pursued by many of their contemporaries — ones which may ultimately provide yet further possibilities for the personal negotiation of contexts, occasions and systems of meaning. In such ways we can see the continuing development of accomplishment by which very special competences and subjectivities come to inhere with subjects such as those involved in the present research.

Affirmation and Challenge Within the Choice of Curricular Options

We have seen that there were a number of reasons why respondents attended GCE Advanced level classes at Spatown College rather than the sixth-forms of local schools. Some of these related to the personal autonomy that respondents felt they would be given within a College context. Others related more to the antipathy students displayed towards curricular options and dominant pedagogic strategies in schools.

> ... There were lots of reasons really (why I went to College), I hated school as you know, but also you could do subjects there (College) which you couldn't do at school — things like history of art. I mean ... and there were chances to really experiment with your art which you couldn't do at school ... (*Jill*, Inteview, October 1981)

> ... and I knew that I didn't want to do 'A' levels at school. I didn't want to do an 'A' level in ancient history from a really

Table 3: GCE Advanced level subjects studied by students

Subject	Number of students studying this subject throughout the fieldwork
English literature	19
History of art	16
Art	15
Sociology	12
Communication studies	10
Theatre studies	7
Languages	4
History	3
Psychology	2
Science subjects	2
Geography	1
Mathematics	0

boring teacher at school who would just dictate notes at you for forty minutes, and I felt that I did want to do 'A' levels. I felt that if I could choose what I wanted to do, then I would enjoy it a bit more ... (*Carol*, Interview, March 1981)

Once at Spatown College, however, students were very selective in their choice of GCE subjects (table 3). English literature, history of art, art, sociology, communication studies and theatre studies were popular options, whereas more scientific and mathematically-oriented subjects were less frequently chosen.

It is possible to detect some degree of homology between the curricular options preferred by students and those *culturally acceptable* forms of experience valued within homes. GCE subjects such as English literature, art, history of art and theatre studies provide opportunities for personal acquaintance with historically and culturally exotic art forms, plays and literature. Furthermore, they are those subjects most likely to give credit to personal reactions to what is being studied.

Students' curricular choices were also influenced by their negative evaluation of other options on offer at College. Many male respondents negatively evaluated their contemporaries who were undertaking industrial training or courses in building or engineering at Spatown College. These negative evaluations often emphasized definitions of sexuality; in particular, around definitions of manliness.

... They're all so macho those engineering 'lads' (sneer). All they ever do is go around getting pissed and trying to pick up secretaries (female students following courses of secretarial training at College). They're sort of really thick and brutish and boring ... (*Ric*, Fieldnotes, July 1981)

... You should see Brett in the common room (at College). He just walks around showing off his biceps and thinking he's really big because he does weight training and is a brickie (students following courses in bricklaying at College). So fucking big he thinks he is, but he's really stupid in fact ... (*Phil*, Fieldnotes, July 1981)

Those male students who worked seriously on GCE courses at College were also negatively evaluated by male respondents, although in a somewhat different way.

... Bill? He just wants to go to university and do really well. He sits around in the library all the time ... gets his essays in on time. But he misses so much, never goes out in the evenings. You wouldn't catch him up the 'Roundhouse'. He must have a really boring life in fact ...
... What do you mean by boring? (PA)
... Well, he must ... I mean, he doesn't go out with women, does he? I mean, he's a bit of a wanker really ... (*Jim*, Fieldnotes, September 1981)

In the light of comments such as these it would seem that male students in the present study perceived themselves as intermediate between those who were excessively 'macho' in their sexual style and those who were essentially 'sexless'. When asked directly about their own sexuality, they tended to emphasize their ability to be more 'successful' than either of the two other groups in their sexual relationships with females.

... I mean ... the thing that makes us different from the brickies is that they're always after it, whereas we get it more often ...
... What? (PA)
... Well, they're always prowling around together trying to pick up women, and usually getting too pissed to do it in the process, whereas we get women much more easily ...
... Why do you think that is? (PA)
... Well, probably because of the way we look, the fact that we talk to women and listen to them, things like that ... (*Ric*, Fieldnotes, March 1982)

Such a conception of manliness, operating with an understanding of the self as heterosexually more 'successful' than either hard working students who 'never have it' or brickies who were so busy 'looking for it' that they rarely 'got it', is important since it shows that in terms of their heterosexual expression, male students located themselves somewhere in between the brutish manliness they associated with manual labour and the essential impotence they saw as characteristic of those whose involvement in mental labour was both committed and industrious. These evaluations had consequences for male students' academic achievement. Because of the negative associations it held for them, male students rarely applied themselves to academic study in any sustained way. To do so ran the risk of being perceived by others as 'wimpish' or 'wet'. Instead, males cultivated a relationship with academic work in which the display of *effortless achievement* was central. Many acted as if their own intrinsic talents alone would ensure success in GCE examinations. Notes were rarely, if ever, taken in class, set work was seldom completed and lectures were for the large part sporadically attended. In consequence, it is perhaps little surprise that male students' academic attainment was low. Six failed to gain any passes at GCE Advanced level and of the rest, few had obtained other than bare pass grades by the time they left College.

Female students on the other hand drew clear distinctions between themselves and contemporaries who had left school at 16 to get engaged, marry and 'settle down'.

> ... But our other friend from the same road, she's got married now and is buying a house in Radstone, and she came round to me the other day and it was so awful because she was so restrained and faithful to her husband. She won't say a word against him and preserves this honeymoon existence. And they talk to each other in these silly voices all the time. They never seem to use their normal voices. She doesn't seem to know anything about people. There's just her and the baby and they go and visit the mother-in-law and things like that. It's so awful to end up like that. I couldn't do it ... (*Elaine*, Interview, October 1981)

They also perceived themselves differently from those who had stayed on at school for further GCE study. Their negative evaluation of this course of action was one which equated staying on at school with a concern to enter traditionally 'feminine' fields of employment such as nursing or office work. Contemporaries who stayed on at school were perceived as too readily acquiescing to teachers' expectations about the sorts of paid employment women should undertake. As Brenda commented,

> ... They (the teachers) never used to allow anybody to expand on what they wanted to do ...
>
> ... How do you mean? (PA)
>
> ... Well I used to get ... they used to mock my theory that I wanted to go into the theatre and change it. And I think they wanted basically nurses and secretaries to come out of the school, and for anyone to do anything else and be even slightly enterprising was very difficult ... So the best thing to do was to actually leave and go somewhere else. They were all very prim in the sixth-form. They were the sort of people who weren't prepared to do anything else. They stuck to the school system right the way through ... (*Brenda*, Interview, January 1981)

Those female students at Spatown College who worked hard for GCE study were also looked down upon by female respondents. Their actions, too, were evaluated in terms of the extent to which they too readily conformed to dominant images of femininity.

> ... Oh Sheila and Vi, they're so disgustingly twee. They're always creeping around the library, working hard on their essays and things like that, wearing those disgusting pretty skirts with flowers on them, drinking dry martinis and orange juices in the pub. They're just vile. They're always giggling and blushing. Urk ... (*Wendy*, Fieldnotes, March 1981)

However, students like Sheila and Vi were denigrated not simply because of their 'pretty skirts' and their 'giggling and blushing' but because of their willingness to 'work hard' in the library. Throughout the study there was ample evidence that both female and male respondents evaluated those who achieved academically without apparent effort more positively than those who did so by 'working hard'.

Interestingly enough, students following courses of secretarial training at Spatown College were also looked down upon by female respondents.

> ... And it (the common room at College) was taken over by other sections, people from the other side, secretaries, they rather took it over.
>
> ... What was wrong with that? (PA)
>
> ... We didn't want to be associated with them.
>
> ... Why not? (PA)
>
> ... Well, we looked down on the secretaries and catering students. They were only doing it to get jobs which were

really boring. They're going to go and get some shitty job which pays £30 a week and that's it. I think we felt that we were more liberated than them, and that our horizons were wider. And they were all so feminine ... (*Norma*, Interview, March 1981)

These negatively evaluated images of women's involvement in education contrasted sharply with the self evaluations of respondents themselves.

... I think that we felt we were more broadminded. I think we all sort of presumed that we would be going to university or polytechnic or something, sort of higher education. We had that sort of attitude, and they didn't. You know ... I took it for granted that was what I was going to do. You know ... I wasn't thinking about work or a job or anything like that ... (*Carol*, Interview, March 1981)

Higher educational experience, particularly that to be gained through the study of the fine arts and humanities, was more positively evaluated by female respondents. When I asked Carol why she had first wanted to undertake GCE advanced level study, she commented,

... To learn, to live, to change ... new experiences ... (*Carol*, Interview, March 1981)

In making such a choice, she perceived clear differences between her own aspirations and those of her contemporaries who had stayed on at school.

... Yes, well I haven't been brought up to think of work like that, of being a secretary or working in a factory or something like that. I feel my aspirations are higher and have been given to think that I can do something in another world separate from the physical world ... (*Carol*, Interview, March 1981)

Susan, Barbara and Jane also expressed a wish to study at art school after leaving college. Petra, Jill, Carol and Wendy intended studying the arts and humanities at polytechnic or university, and Brenda intended going to drama school. For all of them, these intentions were linked to future employment aspirations. Both Jill and Carol, for example, shared an interest in literature which led them to see possible careers for themselves in the world of publishing.

... What would you like to do? (PA)
... I'd like to do something like read on the radio or read

books prior to publication, something like that. I'd like to live somewhere really nice and read books ... (*Jill*, Interview, September 1981)

... Well ... I'd like to write, to be able to write well. Maybe that's a career, and maybe live by it ... (*Carol*, Interview, May 1981)

Similarly, Barbara, Susan and Jane thought that one day they might work in employment associated with fine art.

... Do you ever think you'll have a paid job? (PA)
... I don't know ... because if I do the Foundation course (at art school). At the moment I would like to do sculpture. But when I do the Foundation course I might do something else like graphics. I think that if I went to art school, I would choose something that I knew I could get a job with easily, you know, even if I knew that I didn't want to do it too much ... (*Barbara*, Interview, October 1981)

... What sort of job would you like? (PA)
... Well, I'll be my own boss. That's what I would want to be. I could never be bossed around by someone else. I would hate that. I could never be told what to do because of my parents. Well ... my Mum. They never told me what to do. I would like to paint, make furniture perhaps ... things like that ... (*Susan*, Interview, December 1981)

The antipathy which female students showed towards domestic labour, office and shop work, and committed academic study placed them in a somewhat ambiguous position. On the one hand, because they thought they were likely to go on to higher education, female students valued their time at college since 'A' level success would provide them with the means by which to fulfil such ambitions. On the other, because they negatively evaluated those who 'worked hard' in the pursuit of academic goals, their commitment to the courses on which they were enrolled was weak. As would be expected, the resolution of tensions such as these had profound consequences for overall levels of academic attainment. Of the fourteen female respondents involved in this study, six left College with no qualifications additional to those they possessed on enrolment and amongst those that passed GCE Advanced level examinations, few obtained a higher grade than E (the lowest grade qualifying for a pass).

For female and male respondents, therefore, subject choice at College was influenced both by home-based affirmations and by the rejection of masculinities and femininities associated with other forms of study. Furthermore, processes of affirmation and challenge not only determined students' choice of courses but also the relatively uncommitted way in which academic study came subsequently to be pursued.

The manner in which students negotiated their secondary and College education also had consequences of a more far-reaching nature. Because students chose to study subjects which affirmed the kinds of *culturally acceptable* experience they had encountered at home, and because their career ambitions lay in spheres of practice associated with the dissemination and control of systems of meaning (the fine, media and theatre arts), it is possible to identify aspects of their social practice which *culturally reproduce* their parents' concern to exert control over cultural meanings. Students differed from their parents though in terms of the nature of their commitment to academic study. Whereas their parents' involvement in academic study had been for the large part committed and industrious (thirty-two out of forty of them had degrees or teaching diplomas), students were profoundly suspicious of any display of academic commitment. For them, a work ethic which emphasized personal style and a display of *effortless achievement* was much more highly valued.

Beneath these surface commitments, however, were more fundamental principles influencing students' understanding of the importance of academic study. When asked to reflect on their experience at Spatown College, many of them described somewhat ambivalently the 'lack of structure' they had encountered there.

> ... In some ways I think it was all too loose. I mean ... we were never really made to work ... I think that's a bad thing in some ways because we could have done so much more if we'd been made to do that ... (*Jill*, Interview, September 1981)

> ... When I think of a lot of Petra's friends, they all went to public school and that, like Spatown High, and they were all taught how to study. You know, they all just sit down and read books for fun and watch Shakespeare plays and comment about them, things like that. I mean ... they've actually learned how to study and I haven't. I'd really like to go back and start all over again ... (*Susan*, Interview, July 1982)

There is evidence here of some tension between a cultural style which rejects diligence and effort in the pursuit of academic goals, and respondents' recognition that being 'made to work' and being 'taught how to study' may make academic success more likely.

Affirmation and Challenge Towards Involvement in Sport

Throughout their school and college experience, students displayed marked antipathy towards participation in team-based sport. For many of them, this rejection was closely related to ideologies linking involvement in this kind of sport with competitiveness.

> ... I mean ... no one could appreciate that the reason why I didn't want to play football wasn't because I didn't want to be with a load of yobs ... I mean working class yobs ... It was because it wasn't part of my social life really. It was because I was interested in other things like drawing and writing. I never learned the skills really to compete. And I didn't like the idea of that sort of competition anyway ... (*Dave*, Interview, March 1981)

> ... Why didn't you do games? (PA)
> ... I think it was the competitive side of things that I didn't like, because doing games is very competitive isn't it? The only thing I find vaguely interesting is watching gymnastics. Well ... because it's more physical. I mean ... visually, gymnastics is much more interesting to look at than cricket, say. It's nicer to watch and also it's not so competitive as other things ... (*Jane*, Interview, September 1981)

Competitive team-based sports were also rejected because they were perceived as lacking in cultural grace. In contrast, individual sports such as gymnastics, tennis, snooker and swimming were more positively evaluated, partly because they were perceived as having a certain aesthetic precision,

> ... I love watching snooker though. I really enjoy that ... because it's so satisfying, it's so neat and precise ... (*Carol*, Interview, March 1981)

but also because of certain of their social connotations.

> ... Well they (Dave's parents) always played tennis. They were brilliant at tennis. Dad always wanted me to take up

tennis. He said it was so ... it would ease your socialization, your socialization with other people. I mean ... it would be a good middle class skill to have ... (*Dave*, Interview, February 1981)

Only a few students had shown any real involvement in team-based sport throughout their secondary education, and they too had come to reject this by the time of the fieldwork. In explaining why they had given up this type of activity, reference was frequently made to the constraints that participation in organized sport put on their use of time.

... I used to be captain of hockey and netball and rounders for the first two years, and then I became totally disinterested in the way they ran the whole system of, you know, the hierarchical system of who gets in what team and that. Then this theatre company started up and I wasn't prepared to give up going to the theatre company when we were going to play a match. I would have rather gone to a rehearsal than have to play a match ... (*Brenda*, Interview, January 1981)

Also contributing to this subsequent rejection of team-based sport by those who had originally participated in it, were the over-zealous efforts of teachers to encourage committed involvement to school teams.

... When I arrived at John Manvers School, the games teacher practically forced me into the hockey team there. Like ... quite often I used to spend my time at lunchtime hiding from her because she would come and look for you and drag you down the hockey pitch. I remember I used to enjoy hockey until she started forcing me into it ... (*Barbara*, Interview, September 1981)

While most students were non-participative in organized team sport, they all expressed an interest in dance and movement. Brenda, Wendy and Carol regularly danced together in the 'Tube Club' and down 'The Dugout'. Dave, Nigel and Phil and Tom also spent a lot of time 'bopping' in such settings. Dave in particular frequently referred to the time when he had entered a disco dance competition 'as a joke' only to end up winning second prize. For many students, creative dance was enjoyable because of its aesthetic connotations.

... I really like dancing a lot. In a way, dancing for me is like art. I get the same feeling from it. That's all that I think about when I'm doing it ... (*Barbara*, Interview, September 1981)

In making sense of students' preferences with respect to involvement in physical activity and sport, it is important to recognize that this too showed elements of both affirmation and challenge. Students' positively evaluated those aspects of organized sport that emphasized personal expression and aesthetic precision (qualities highly prized within their home lives), but rejected those that emphasized group solidarity, physical aggression and overt competition. Dance and movement on the other hand — activities which were perceived as allowing for personal creativity — were the physical activities that students most often referred to as enjoyable. Such forms of expression allow those participating in them considerable autonomy with respect to the production and recontextualization of bodily movements: overall success within them being predicated upon the creation of innovative structures and sequences. Because of this, dance and movement are forms of physical activity that most resonate with respondents' concern for temporal and spatial autonomy. Forms of physical activity imbued with such qualities proved acceptable to students. Rationalized, routinized and regularized physical activity was not. Insights such as these help us make better sense of respondents' descriptions of the few occasions when they did appear to involve themselves in team sports.

> ... Well, the other weekend there were a few of us having a game of football outside the Crescent.
> ... How do you mean? I thought you didn't like playing football (PA)
> ... Well, it wasn't football really. It was just a knock-about. There's not any rules. We were just kicking the ball about.
> ... How do you mean, there weren't any rules? (PA)
> ... Well, we were trying to get the ball past each other but it didn't matter really. I mean ... it didn't matter if you didn't get the ball past each other. It was a laugh really. I really enjoyed it. It *wasn't really football*, just kicking a ball around. It was fun ... (*Phil*, Fieldnotes, April 1981 [emphasis added])

Such a game, which might appear to an outsider to be football was, in Phil's eyes at least, nothing of the sort. The actions might appear to be the same, involving the kicking of a ball in an attempt to get it past others, but the meanings that these actions had for those involved were not those emphasizing group accomplishment. Rather they were ones organized around *personalizing processes* associated with 'having a laugh', 'kicking a ball around' and 'trying to get the ball past each other'.

Finally, we can find parallels between students' antipathy towards organized team sport and their attempts to challenge other aspects of the schooling process. Brenda's opting out of sport, for example, only took place after she had been 'practically forced into the school hockey team'. If, as was argued earlier, respondents were concerned, by virtue of their home experience, to challenge contexts which were strongly framed, then their hostility towards teachers' attempts to involve them in school teams can be seen as yet further consequences of the disjunction between principles of control operating in the home and at school.

Summary

In this chapter, I have tried to show how students' negotiation of educational contexts was, to a large extent, influenced by the transportation of practices from the home to the educational site of experience. In particular, I have argued that better sense can be made of respondents' challenges to aspects of secondary schooling which did not allow them personal autonomy, if we see these as contestations arising from a disjunction between the framing of experience at home and at school.

The transition from secondary school to college of further education was therefore motivated both by an antipathy towards those aspects of secondary schooling which restricted personal freedom and by a desire to undertake further academic study in an environment perceived as likely to encourage personal autonomy. By making this transition, students attempted to relocate themselves educationally in an environment where principles of control were more likely to mirror those within the home.

Additionally, the transportation of the strong classificatory relationship between *culturally acceptable* and *culturally non-acceptable* forms of experience from home to college, had the effect of encouraging students to devalue certain curricular options. Subjects which failed to conform to criteria of cultural worth operating in the home were rarely studied. Furthermore, because opportunities for personalizing involvement in academic study operate discontinuously even within preferred subjects, and because *effortless achievement* was so highly valued by students, their chances of examination success remained limited.

Finally in this chapter I have tried to show how students' educational experience helped reinforce not only specific forms of cultural arbitrariness affirmed within the home, but also strategies of inter-personal communication concerned with personal justification and the control of systems of meaning. Throughout their time at College, students thereby consolidate their competence to distinguish between differing degrees of culturally arbitrary worth as well as their ability to use more general strategies of cultural imposition.

Chapter 5

Sub-culture

Introduction

In the previous two chapters I argued that as a result of their home and educational experience, students came to be able to differentiate between *culturally acceptable* and *culturally non-acceptable* realms of experience. I also suggested that the strong classificatory relationship between these two spheres of practice was established both by a selective bringing together of elements of public and private experience within the home and by the manner in which respondents subsequently negotiated their school and college experience. As a result of this, criteria of *authenticity* came to be established which enabled students to differentiate cultural activities which allow for personal creativity and control over systems of meanings from those which do not. Within the former category of practice were activities associated with the fine and mediated arts and with those aspects of social and communication studies which allow personalized application.

In this chapter 1 will explore some of the consequences of these processes for the nature of students' *sub-cultural* experience. In using the term sub-cultural experience, I intend to identify a sphere of practice consisting of a number of specialized social, spatial and temporal contexts which are relatively 'hidden' from parental and teacherly surveillance. Some of these contexts, such as the flats and bedsits used by students, were entirely free from adult scrutiny. Others were more public contexts over which some surveillance was possible. Spatown Arts Centre, for example, was regularly used as a meeting place by both students and their parents. On the other hand, whilst many of the public houses and nightclubs popular among students were formally accessible to parents, few were visited because of preconceptions the latter held about them.

... You wouldn't catch me gadding about in 'The Round-house'. What with all those underage kids getting drunk all over the place ... (*Mr Cooper*, Fieldnotes, March 1981)

At first sight, comments like these did not seem to match the observations I had made in students' homes where, it will be recalled, a large amount of time was spent by parents talking with their daughters' and sons' friends. These contradictions suggested that invisible screening within the home did not have a direct counterpart at the sub-cultural site. Fieldwork, however, revealed that in sub-cultural settings, direct invisible screening had its equivalent in more covert forms of surveillance. Some parents, for example, knew the landlord of 'The Roundhouse' as a personal friend who often attended their own parties. Others knew the Director of Spatown Arts Centre and the Administrator of Spatown Youth Theatre. Furthermore, some parents served on the Management Committee of the local authority Youth Centre in which Spatown Youth Theatre was situated, Amateur drama productions, in which many parents were involved, were also staged in this Youth Centre. By using gossip networks associated with these settings, parents were thereby able to exert indirect surveillance over students' sub-cultural practices.

In analyzing student activity at this site I shall begin by describing three specific sub-cultural contexts regarded as important by all those interviewed — 'The Roundhouse', Spatown Arts Centre and Spatown Youth Theatre.

Preferred Sites, Preferred Practices

One of the most popular sub-cultural sites was a public house called 'The Roundhouse'. Consisting of two adjacent bars surrounding a central serving area, 'The Roundhouse' was located in a Georgian building in the centre of Spatown. Students remembered having met here regularly since leaving school. Friday and Saturday evenings were occasions when the largest number of respondents were likely to be present, but Christmas, Easter and summer vacations were also popular times for reunions with friends temporarily away from the city.

One of the most distinctive features of 'The Roundhouse' was its open-plan design. Spatially, it had been constructed so that there were a number of alcoves and separate conversation areas from which it was possible to observe others, check out who people arrived with and who, throughout the evening, talked with who. For students, 'The Roundhouse' had been an important, if somewhat ambivalently regarded, meeting place for a long time.

> ... What was it about it ('The Roundhouse') that you liked? (PA)
> ... It was full of young people and the nice thing about 'The Roundhouse' is that so many different kinds of people went there. Even though they were young and a lot of them were students, you had so many different kinds in there. Like there was the grockle crowd. Then there was the hippie crowd. Then there was the 'Clique'. Then there was the University (lot). Then there were gangs of women, you know, secretarial types. If you went to 'The Roundhouse' then you found out where the parties were. It was just where everybody met actually ... (*Wendy*, Interview, March 1981)

> ... Lots of people of the same age used to go there. Well, it obviously did become a centre (of activity). It sort of became the place where, if there was a party, then that was where you could find it in our circle I suppose. I don't know, because we used to complain about it all the time. But it became a habit. And if you didn't go there on Saturday then you felt that you'd fucked the whole week up. That you'd missed out on something. God knows what. Something to change your life ... (*Phil*, Interview, March 1981)

For many students, 'The Roundhouse' was a friendly and informal place in which to meet. Not only did its landlord allow underage drinking to take place, but by going there it was always possible to find out where the best parties were going to be later that night. For female students, 'The Roundhouse' was also important for other reasons too since, within it, they had first begun to explore together the nature of feminist political commitment.

> ... In my second year (at Spatown College) I used to adore it. I loved every minute of it. From September right the way through. I mean ... there were unhappy moments, but I really liked it. It was really nice being there with a group of women ...
> ... So what were the really good things about it? (PA)
> ... Well ... I discovered left-wing politics. I had these new girlfriends. We found feminism and I finally got out of the

horrible places I used to go to ... (*Patsie*, Interview, February 1981)

... What did you used to do in 'The Roundhouse'? (PA)
... We used to chat about politics and things. They weren't unintelligible conversations ... We were trying to get our political ideas together and the things we believed in. And then we moved on from that to talk about Womens' Liberation, and had vicious fights with men across the room ... (*Wendy*, Interview, January 1981)

The developing feminist consciousness of female students had important consequences subculturally not only for themselves but for men in 'The Roundhouse'. As Brenda explained,

... Well ... Carol used to stomp across the room and hit men over the head ...
... Why? (PA)
... Well, somebody would make a sexist remark or something. She would walk across the room and have an argument with them. We used to go out and have arguments with blokes and things, became known as the sweatshirt girls. And we would get men coming up to us and saying 'Do you know, someone told us you were lesbians'. (*Brenda*, Interview, January 1981)

The Roundhouse's most positively evaluated characteristics included its popularity with local University and Polytechnic students and the opportunities it afforded to meet 'new and interesting' people.

... It was a sort of wonderful fantasy, you know, you would go down the pub and you would think that you were going to have a really fantastic time, and you were going to meet all these new and interesting people, and that it was all going to be different ... (*Carol*, Interview, March 1981)

'Interesting' people were defined in a variety of ways, but the majority of such definitions emphasized their likely acquaintance with, and ability to talk about, books, films, theatre, politics and music.

... An interesting person for me would be someone who could actually talk about what they had been reading recently, and would talk about it, films and things like that ... (*Carol*, Interview, March 1981)

... they'd be into going to see bands and things, would have
experiences and things which they could talk about, would
know about film, could talk about it, wouldn't be static ...
(*Ric*, Interview, July 1981)

'The Roundhouse' was also a context in which other people could
be gossipped and talked about. This was facilitated both by its open-
plan design which allowed ample opportunity for the surveillance of
others, and by respondents' desire to exert personal control over the
social identities of friends and acquaintances. Within the context of
previous discussion relating to the home and educational experience of
respondents, there are a number of interesting parallels between practices at this site and others. Indirect screening by the landlord meant
that many of those present were subjected to surveillance by at least
one person close to their parents. The physical openness of the context, as well as gossip about others, enabled respondents to monitor
the practices of those around them. The public discussion of political
issues and personal stances with respect to these also shares some
similarity with the nature of talk within the home.

Another popular sub-cultural context, until its closure in the
middle of 1981, was Spatown Arts Centre. This consisted of a book-
shop, a foodstore, a gallery and a large multi-purpose hall which was
used as a cafe during the day and as for theatre and cinema presenta-
tions in the evening. On the whole, respondents' social practices in
this context centred around the large open hall which contained clusters of second-hand armchairs and settees, recovered with sailcloth
and painted in brilliant colours. Coffee and various wholefoods were
served in this area during the day where it was possible to sit and talk
undisturbed for relatively long periods of time.

Spatown Arts Centre was administered by a local entrepreneur,
well-known to students and their parents. For a time it was the only
place locally where it was possible to see foreign films unlikely to be
shown in commercial cinemas. Modern dance, mime and theatre
groups performed there regularly, and evening classes were offered
in meditation, movement and yoga. When I asked respondents what
attracted them to the centre, their responses were similar to those they
gave about 'The Roundhouse'.

... So who did you know that used to go there? (PA)
... People like Petra, Jill, that crowd. I didn't know Ruth at
the time. Who else did I know? Well yes, I did know quite a
few people. But I mean, I just thought that I would meet new

people, and it would be more exciting to go there, and I did
... (*Norma*, Interview, June 1981)

> ... What did you used to do down the Arts Centre? (PA)
> ... You used to just sit around and chat and smoke. No, that
> was a good time for me when I went to College. Spatown
> Arts Centre was good because all the good films that I've seen
> used to be on there. Otherwise, you don't get good films
> unless you go to Broadville. I saw *Satyricon* which was good
> ... just films that you don't get to see elsewhere ... (*Phil*,
> Interview, September 1981)

Within this context too, students felt they might meet 'new' and potentially 'exciting' people. Stuart, for example, explicitly likened aspects of Spatown Arts Centre to 'The Roundhouse'.

> ... What did you think about the Arts Centre? (PA)
> ... Well, that again was a bit like 'The Roundhouse', you
> know? It was just a place where you went to see what was
> going on, and to be seen. It was very cliquey. But it was good
> actually. It was a lovely place and a good meeting place. And
> it was a nice place to go and sit. Say you were on your own, it
> was a nice place to go and sit and have coffee. There was
> always someone to watch. I could do that for hours ...
> (*Stuart*, Interview, July 1981)

Another popular site was Spatown Youth Centre with its associated youth theatre and drop-in cafe. As I have already mentioned, a number of parents were members of the Management Committee of the Youth Centre and others took part in amateur dramatic and operatic productions staged at it. After Spatown Arts Centre closed in mid 1981, the drop-in cafe at the Youth Centre took its place as the students' principal day-time meeting place.

> ... It was the sort of place where you could go and sit. You
> could talk, meet people, find out what was going on. We used
> to go there at lunchtime, rather than eat in the shitty refectory
> at College ... (*Norma*, Interview, June 1981)

Nine students belonged to the youth theatre whose productions were staged in the youth centre and this too was an important social focus for sub-cultural activity. Respondents felt that they had gained a lot in terms of personal development from involvement in its productions. Some went so far as to talk of having discovered unrealized personal potentials during their theatre work.

> ... I was 15 and there was this pantomine and the rehearsals started in September of that year. But I didn't really want to go because ... maybe I was too shy and I didn't want to act and things like that. And they were doing rehearsals and then suddenly this person who was doing the main part — Buttons — decided to pull out. Yeah ... and he decided he didn't want to do it. And I went along and I knew I couldn't do it because I was so embarrassed at that time about reading aloud. I just couldn't read the words. I've never felt so ill. But then I read the script and I got on the stage and I played Buttons and another character, and suddenly I found I could actually speak in public. And I had to sing a song, and I thought, 'God, where has all this come from?' ... (*Nigel*, Interview, December 1981)

But involvement in Spatown Youth Theatre also had consequences for students' responses to schooling.

> ... Well, I was 13, 12 or 13. I can't remember exactly how old I was. Paul Sullivan and a couple of us, well about ten of us, started Spatown Youth Theatre and for about three years we used to run just pantomimes and things ... and then it sort of expanded and the trouble started at school because I wanted to do that as opposed to doing CSEs, reading books which I found were not interesting ... and they weren't prepared to examine anything else. They were only prepared to examine the CSE syllabus and you used to get to places where you wanted to read other things ... (*Brenda*, Interview, January 1981)

In Brenda's comments a clear contrast is drawn between her experience of school which she found personally restricting and her work in the youth theatre. Another aspect of the youth theatre which was frequently mentioned was the charismatic flair of its Administrator — Rupert Wilde — who, in addition to his professional responsibilities, held after-rehearsal parties and meetings at his flat.

> ... Well ... he sort of had a fascination for me at that age. Because at that age you're very impressionable and being like he was, I was very impressed by it. Not impressed. Well, yes, impressed. You know, homosexual, bisexual or whatever ...

and it was all sort of ... Anyway, it started at these parties. We used to have these parties after rehearsals and got very drunk and things like that ... and he had this sort of charisma ... (*Nigel*, Interview, December 1981)

... Oh, it was weird, but it was such good fun. A lot of people all together who liked each other ... It was, we were only 15 or 16, but it was such good fun. And with Rupert sort of presiding over us. I'm sure that all of us who were involved in that would have been quite different people if we hadn't met Rupert. ... We used to go there about twice a week and spend our evenings talking about things — politics, films, people. We never really ... I mean the plays we did ... It was just those meetings ... (*Jill*, Interview, September 1981)

It would appear from the above comments that one of the most valued aspects of the youth theatre was the chance it offered students to become involved in personalized modes of expression such as acting, dancing, designing and music making. In contrast to the educational site of experience, which had for the large part offered relatively closed and non-personally negotiable options, the sub-cultural sites preferred by respondents would appear to have been those offering negotiable and weakly framed alternatives.

While we can gain a great deal of insight into students' lives outside of home and college by identifying the sub-cultural contexts and practices they preferred, a fuller understanding of the dynamics of sub-cultural choice can only be obtained if we compare these with those that were less popular. Some of the most frequently commented upon non-preferred contexts in Spatown were mainstream commercial discotheques and nightclubs. Students' rejection of these was premised on two distinct qualities that they attributed to them. First, a number of females negatively evaluated these contexts because of the association they had with their own early adolescent experience.

... Would you ever go to 'The Mecca'? (PA)
... Oh my god, no! That was where we used to go when we were about 15. Get dressed up on a Friday night and go down there, wear high heel shoes and things. It was disgusting really, now that I think about it. All that make-up. All that waste! No, I like to think that's all behind me now ... (*Carol*, Interview, March 1981)

... I mean ... I was going to places like 'Snoopy's' and 'The

Mecca' when I was about 15. I wouldn't go there now. The men we used to go with were bricklayers and things like that, and I didn't have a boyfriend ... (*Lennie*, Interview, February 1981)

Secondly, both female and male respondents rejected social settings like these because of the positionality which participation in them required. Females, in particular, commented on the effects that dominant expectations about female and male roles in mainstream discotheques had for their autonomy as women.

... Well ... I don't think that discos like that are much fun really, where everybody just has to. I mean ... they're just like cattle markets really, I think. The women are all wearing very pretty dresses and the men are all up at the bar getting pissed. And then, a nice little dance to something really horrid, like Boney M, something like that. But I've never been able to see what they're really for actually ... (*Carol*, Interview, March 1981)

'... Well ... like I say, I think the majority of those secretarial type women, their sole aim of going to 'The Mecca' was in order to get picked up. Which I suppose is what discos and parties are for in a way. But having it thrust upon you like that was a bit much ... (*Susan*, Interview, February 1981)

Male students, however, were somewhat more ambivalent in their attitudes towards these settings. Some indicated that they enjoyed going to them because they offered them the chance to dance. At the same time, however, when they were in commercial discotheques, male students showed some apprehension about the possibility that, for them, an evening out could easily end in violence.

... I like going to 'Snoopy's' sometimes because you can have a good dance there. But it's the sort of place where ... you sometimes feel uneasy all the time because you never know when someone's going to come up and ... when some yobbo brickie type is going to start something. You know ... sometimes you can't even smile at people because they will take it the wrong way ... (*Phil*, Fieldnotes, April 1981)

Male students also expressed anxiety about the pressures on them to conform to dominant ideologies governing male behaviour in such contexts.

> ... The trouble with going to discos and things like that is
> that everyone's expected to behave in a certain way. You
> know, the women are always together in groups, and then
> we're supposed to go over and chat them up. It's all so stupid
> really, I think ... (*Ric*, Interview, May 1981)

In contrast to preferred sub-cultural settings, Spatown's mainstream discotheques and nightclubs were those which allowed students limited personal autonomy; being contexts in which gendered
modes of practice in particular were relatively pre-given and non-
negotiable. In the light of this, we can extend our analysis of preferred
sites for sub-cultural practice to suggest that, by and large, these were
those that were weakly framed. They were also environments in
which students had significant control over meanings within them.
Processes as apparently diverse as the public debating of personal
political commitments, the presentation of the self in new ways
through role play and acting, the design and management of staged
theatrical productions and gossip about others, share certain features
in common, being social practices organized around the personal
control of systems of meaning. In the case of gossip, the meanings
concerned are attributed as qualities of other people. In the case of
public political debate, the meanings involved are usually self-
referenced. In theatre, art and performance, the social meanings concerned are generally provided for others in commodified and pre-
packaged ways.

The types of sub-cultural activity so far described are significant
in so far as they represent attempts to exert personal control over
social meanings. Their centrality within the dynamics of students'
sub-cultural practice was such that they could be witnessed even in
non-preferred settings. Their existence provides powerful evidence
once again of cultural effects arising from the transportation of practices across sites of experience. It would seem therefore that parents'
efforts to encourage personal autonomy in their daughters and sons
had effects not only educationally but sub-culturally as well. Indeed,
students' efforts to exert personal influence over dominant systems of
meaning extended to those settings which were generally unpopular
as meeting places.

> ... I remember the time when Ann and I went down the
> 'Mecca' at a fancy dress party, and we were so pissed off with
> everyone else that we started smooching together ourselves.
> Then these bouncers appeared and got angry with us and
> chucked us out ... (*Elaine*, Interview, September 1981)

From this brief analysis of sites and practices preferred by students, it would appear that processes of attempted social redefinition were central within respondents' sub-cultural practice. In the next two sections, these social strategies will be examined in more detail.

Re-defining the Public Sphere of Practice

As we have seen, preferred contexts for students were those which allowed high levels of personal autonomy with respect to the negotiation of spatial and temporal possibilities. Other more mundane settings also provided respondents with opportunities to attempt a re-definition of their quality and character. Throughout the fieldwork, three particular dramatic illustrations of this took place.

'It's the Street, But Not Really the Street'

A well documented quality of many youth sub-cultures concerns the way in wich their members 'hang around', 'doss' and otherwise use street areas in town centres as spaces of focal importance for sub-cultural activity (Corrigan, 1979; Willis, 1984). The sub-cultural practice of respondents in this study was no exception in this respect. Throughout the fieldwork, I observed a number of instances of *street bricolage* — attempts by students to re-define the meaning and nature of Spatown street life. Two rather different sets of practices were observed. The first of these was associated with social meetings outside local cafes and public houses. The second concerned more specifically the efforts students made to 'mess around' 'having a laugh' on the street.

Two key sites where respondents would gather during the day were a seating area immediately outside 'The Roundhouse' and the pavement outside 'Snoopy's Club'. Both of these sites were in the centre of the city and afforded a clear view of people walking along Spatown's two main streets. When students were asked why they met at these sites, similar types of response were forthcoming.

> ... Well, it's nice to be there and see what's going on.
> ... How do you mean, what's going on? (PA)
> ... Well, you can see who's with who, who's around. I don't know, things like that ... (*Phil*, Fieldnotes, July 1981)

... It's so nice to be in the open air really. And Spatown is so beautiful. I mean, you can sit there and watch people going by. It's almost like being in another country — Venice — Piazza San Marco — something like that ... (*Jill*, Fieldnotes, June 1982)

A number of interrelated themes are articulated in the above descriptions. First, students were concerned to keep under surveillance the practices of others around them, particularly those of friends and acquaintances. Second, they seemed concerned to imagine that the locations in which their observations took place were somehow more foreign and exotic than they really were. This desire to romanticize everyday situations was further displayed by Jill's behaviour on one occasion when she arrived by taxi with her boyfriend to claim supplementary benefit.

... You should have seen Jill down the dole today. She had this amazing fifties cocktail dress on, black stockings, a hat and veil. She just looked incredible. And there was little Phil beside her, dressed like something out of a Somerset Maugham book — white cotton jacket, baggies, the lot ... The people behind the counter just couldn't believe her. And she arrived in a taxi! (*Dave*, Interview, September 1981)

When I questioned Jill herself about this incident, she commented,

... Honestly, I think the dole is such a boring place that you have to liven things up there. I mean, you might as well bring some style into the place ... It's so dull and boring otherwise ... (*Jill*, Fieldnotes, May 1982)

Other street practices took the form of what might loosely be called 'messing around' in public places. When I asked Jane, for example, why she felt that some of her friends might be considered a little strange, she replied,

... Because they act strange and do strange things. They do silly things like messing around. Like a friend of mine got this umbrella the other day, this really big umbrella and it was really huge, about fifteen feet in diameter. And we were just walking about with that. About twelve people under this fifteen foot umbrella. And I think that an awful lot of people would think that was strange. . . . And if it rains, not worrying, walking down the street with plastic bags on your head to keep the rain off. I mean, a lot of things that I would do and my friends would do, would be very practical but a lot of other people wouldn't do them because they would look strange and funny. Like walking down the street with no shoes on in summer, because in summer you get too hot feet if you've got shoes on ... (*Jane*, Interview, September 1981)

Demonstrated in street practice such as this is students' concern to recontextualize aspects of everyday experience in terms of exoticism or a 'playful', 'couldn't-care-less' spontaneity. Actions like these, by attempting a re-definition of aspects of the public sphere of practice, celebrate personalized control over systems of meaning. Generally speaking, they took the form of *displays to be observed* by others. Street practices such as these also have further implications, since they positioned students where they are able to observe and comment upon other people. They therefore provided access to understandings and information about others which can subsequently be used to authenticate the personalities of others. I shall describe these more fully in the next section of this chapter.

'It's Christmas, But Not Really Christmas'

Early in the fieldwork, an incident occurred which was particularly important as an example of students' attempts to dramatically re-define the meaning of a public situation: it this case, the Christmas Midnight Mass in Spatown Abbey. Barbara described what took place as follows:

> ... I went to the midnight mass on Christmas Eve. We were very drunk so we decided to go to the Abbey. And I was so cross and angry looking around at the people who were obviously sitting there, who said they believed, but obviously would have done fuck all about what they believed, who would obviously never have done anything at all for anybody. And the sight of it made me very cross, and we walked out and made a big scene ...
> ... You made a scene? (PA)
> ... Yeah, well I was drunk and I was cross.
> ... What happened? (PA)
> ... What happened? Well, we were sitting right at the front of the Abbey. Just across from, just right at the front and while we were sitting there I just got crosser and crosser. Then, in

the middle of the communion, I stood up and said, 'Rob, we're leaving this bunch of hypocrites to their religion' and walked out. Right down the aisle of the abbey, making a hell of a noise because there were about twenty of us ... (*Barbara*, Interview, January 1981)

For Barbara and other students present, the Christmas Mass was perceived as lacking authenticity. Indeed, most members of the congregation were perceived as being largely hypocritical in their actions. As Barbara went on to say,

... I could not believe all those people in their nice little suits believing that they were doing some fucking good, and not really caring about anyone except themselves ... (*Barbara*, Interview, January 1981)

The effect of students leaving the Abbey on Christmas Eve was indeed dramatic. As Spatown College's chaplain, who was present at the time, later put it

... We were in the middle of this service and there was this awful noise and then a load of youngsters all marched down the aisle, looking very drunk to me. It was all very embarrassing really. We felt quite sorry for them. At first, we felt that someone had been taken ill at the front but then we saw what was happening ... (*Rev. J. Panting*, Fieldnotes, March 1981)

Given the context and the circumstances, such an challenge to dominant systems of meaning was almost certainly bound to fail. But interestingly enough, Barbara and her friends' presence at the ceremony in the first place would seem to suggest some intentioned desire on their part to attempt a re-definition of the situation since, on a number of previous occasions, considerable antipathy they had displayed towards institutionalized Christian practice.

... I would never get involved with it ... because I don't believe I have to have something like that making restrictions upon my life. Just because someone's written a book called the Bible, or anybody else ... I don't think that any group of people, or person, can make demands on someone else ... (*Barbara*, Interview, January 1981)

In the light of these comments it would seem that student antipathy towards forms of institutionalized Christian practice is once again connected with perceived restraints on personal autonomy.

'*It's Work, But Not Really Work*'

Throughout the fieldwork many respondents obtained part-time paid employment in Spatown. In a number of cases, this was secured through direct or indirect parental intervention and sponsorship. The most popular forms of employment amongst respondents were those in catering and restaurant work. Jill, Susan, Tom and Peter all worked at the 'Alice in Wonderland' restaurant selling burgers and other fast food. Both Wendy and Dave worked at 'Pizza Paradise'. Nigel, Richard, Norma, Barbara, Bill and Dave all worked at 'Uncle Sam's' burger restaurant. Within students' descriptions of their experience working in these contexts, two themes recurred. First, frequent reference was made to the social dimensions of their employment; in particular, the opportunity it afforded to be with friends. Second, respondents commented favourably on the fact that their employers had allowed them to negotiate when and how they worked.

> ... What did you think about 'Uncle Sam's'? (PA)
> ... I suppose I liked it because I made a lot of friends there. And the people I worked for became friends as well. And they let me get on with what I had to do. I wasn't told what I had to do. They treated me as if I knew what I was doing, and they let me get on with it. And also I could get work when I wanted to which was nice ... (*Barbara*, Interview, September 1981)

> ... I think the nice thing about working at the 'Alice' was that you could do what you wanted to do when you wanted to. People accepted me for what I was. And you really got to know people there. Sometimes it was almost as if the customers didn't really matter ... (*Tom*, Fieldnotes, February 1982)

Indeed, personal control over the use of time and the possibility of actually being paid to spend time with friends were themes recurring in students' descriptions of preferred types of employment. This proved to be the case even when the work concerned took place in contexts other than those associated with the restaurant trade.

> ... At one time I got involved with painting this bazaar — lots of little shops. Yeah, that was great fun. I mean, I wouldn't mind doing a job like that because it was so free. You could just go in when you wanted. You could spend all night working and then go to bed all day ... (*Jane*, Interview, September 1981)

Preferred work contexts were therefore those which allowed respondents control over the use of time and the manner in which work was carried out. They were also those which allowed for personalization through acquaintance with new and 'interesting' personal contacts. As Susan commented,

> ... I really look forward to going to the 'Alice' to work sometimes. Especially if you're in the cocktail bar, you can have a really good laugh. Sometimes you get really interesting people in there to talk to. It's not like work really, it's a laugh ... (*Susan*, Fieldnotes, June 1982)

A further quality of preferred work contexts concerned the blurring of distinctions between work and leisure within them. Friends would often drop in for a chat or a drink at the restaurants in which students worked, and students were regular customers in the cocktail bar at the 'Alice in Wonderland' and the late night bar at 'Pizza Paradise' on their nights off work. This transformation of work contexts into personalizing leisure settings had profound consequences for the commercial success of at least one of them. In late 1981, after reputedly having operated at a substantial trading loss for several months, 'Uncle Sam's' was closed by the company which owned it. This closure was in part attributable to the manner in which customers were served. On three separate occasions when I visited this restaurant during the fieldwork, I found it quite impossible to get served because those working there were more interested in talking with friends than serving customers. On other occasions, when food did arrive, it was often cold, ill-prepared and casually served.

So far, by considering processes such as street bricolage, the blurring of distinctions between work and leisure, and intentioned attempts to transform the nature of public ceremonies, I have identified some of the ways in which students attempted to transform the meanings associated with apsects of public social practice in Spatown. I shall now consider the nature and effects of similar principles of attempted transformation at an interpersonal level within more private spheres of practice.

Re-defining the Private Sphere of Practice

Earlier, I pointed out that *gossip about others* was a dominant social practice amongst students. In this section, I will elaborate further on the nature of this social strategy by describing how it was used in students' conversations about each other. I will begin by focussing in particular on the uses to which this form of talk was put by one particular sub-set of respondents before moving to an exploration of the role of gossip about others within the group as a whole.

Amongst male students there was a relatively loose friendship grouping called 'The Clique'. This group had, as its core, seven members — Jim, Bill, Richard, Chris, Brian, Ric and Phil. Throughout the study, these individuals were involved in a variety of sexual relationships with female students. However, from an early stage in the fieldwork it became apparent that the latter regarded the actions of members of 'The Clique' somewhat ambivalently.

... Jim was in my English group and Bill was with Carol at the time. They used to take the piss out of us all the time. They were quite a trendy group and they never used to talk to anybody but themselves. They were very superior. ... I never really used to talk to them much. We just had big rows ...
... What about? (PA)
... Their attitude to women was purely sexual. If you went around with them then you had to sleep with them, and since I wasn't prepared to do that, they used to take the piss out of me, and I used to take the piss back which didn't go down too well. So we used to end up having these huge rows all the time ... (*Wendy*, Interview, February 1981)

Wanda, who for a time shared her flat with Chris and Richard, also held similar views:

... They used to use the flat. ... They all had homes but they also had bedsits where they could hang out. But Richard really felt bad about it because he had a room in my flat and he used to say, 'Why can't I play your record player at three in the morning?' and I would say, 'Because it's my record player and I want to get some sleep.' And they couldn't understand. And they still can't understand why I didn't believe in sitting up all night and taking drugs and getting pissed and then ending up in bed with one of them ... (*Wanda*, Interview, December 1981)

According to a number of respondents, membership of 'The Clique' was structured in such a way that individual members fulfilled certain roles.

... Every person in 'The Clique' would have some sort of function. Like Jim would always be the leader — the leader of

'The Clique'. And someone like Brian, he was the person they
took the piss out of. And everyone sort of had a function, a
role to play. And when they went out together, that was all
they did, they just role played all the time. In a way, it was
like watching a theatre group ... (*Jane*, Interview, September
1981)

A more detailed study of this group and a careful analysis of the
type of comments used by its members to describe other students,
enabled me to identify a distinctive set of communicative strategies
which these male respondents used in public settings. These involved
scrutinizing and commenting disparagingly on the identities, appear-
ances and behaviours of those around them.

... they look to see who's coming in ('The Roundhouse') and
they'll take the piss out of them. And then, they'll take the piss
out of the next one. That's all they can do, pick on other
people's faults to hide their own ... (*Wendy*, Interview,
February 1981)

As the following illustrations of this social strategy show, 'taking
the piss' out of others was a complex process since the objects of
approbation were so diverse.

... Simon is such a pretentious twat. Look at the way he's
standing there next to that shit from 'The Dugout'. He's only
creeping up to him so that he can get in on that scene ... (*Jim*,
Fieldnotes, April 1981)

... Oh come on Rich, don't give me that. Come off it.
You're only talking to her because you fancy her. Don't kid
me you're interested in talking to her about 'Wuthering
Heights' ... (*Bill*, Fieldnotes, February 1981)

Nevertheless, these comments shared a common underlying
structure in that they involved the operation of two distinct moments
in a process by which the identities of others were *personally authenti-
cated*. At the first of these moments, another person's presented identity is systematically deconstructed as false or unreal. At the second,
this is substituted by a reconstructed, more authentic, understanding
of that person. Given the prevalence with which this social strategy
was used, it is little coincidence that the word 'pretentious' was one
of the most frequently employed descriptions used by members of
'The Clique'. The widespread use of this term, which positions the
person using it as an individual with privileged insight into the mo-

tives and practices of those to whom it is attributed, suggests that underlying the use of this social strategy too, were principles connected with the control of systems of meaning.

Whilst these strategies were frequently used by members of 'The Clique', they were also practised by other respondents. Dave, while not himself a member of 'The Clique', showed similar tendencies in his analysis of a Spatown punk who lived in the same street as him.

> ... And as for Steve who plucks his eyebrows by all account. He's a cunt, an arrogant bastard.... I mean, I know it's only because he feels so fucking inadequate in himself, but I don't see why he has to put on that act with me ... (*Dave*, Interview, February 1981)

In the above account, we can see how Steve's presented identity is first deconstructed and then reconstructed so as to suggest that in reality he is personally inadequate. Female students also employed similar social strategies, although they tended to use them less often in public settings.

> ... I mean, the thing about Jill is that she pretends to be a friend of mine ... I mean, really she's just trying to muscle in on what I'm doing. ... She's just trying to use me to get in on what I'm doing. ... She's just trying to use me to get in on my circle of friends ... (*Susan*, Interview, March 1982)

In this account, Susan systematically deconstructs Jill's professed interest in her, reconstructing this to suggest that Jill is simply someone who is 'trying to muscle in' on Susan's own circle of friends. In the following quotation, Susan again deconstructs the presented identity of another respondent, Jane, rejecting her efforts to present herself as independent, and reconstructing her behaviour as indicative of her servility within the relationships she and her friends had with younger boys.

> ... She's got this, she's part of this circle of 20-year-old girls who all have younger boyfriends. I mean, she's quite independent and things. Well, she appears that way. She's got her own car and things like that. But she gets these young boys around her flat and then she sits around while they get stoned, proving their manliness by taking all these strong drugs — sulphate, coke, and things I've never heard of. And she'll go and score for them ... things like that ... (*Susan*, Fieldnotes, May 1982)

Interestingly enough, in an earlier interview, Barbara applied this same analytic strategy to Susan herself.

> ... I find her two-faced really. She'll be nice to you and then say horrible things about you behind your back. And she spends all her time after the Richmonds. That's all she spends her time doing, trying to get off with one of them ... (*Barbara*, Interview, September 1981)

And Peter, in describing those who worked at the 'Alice in Wonderland' had this to say,

> ... I mean ... most of the people who work down the 'Alice', they're social misfits really. I mean, take Jo — she's into saddlery at the moment. I ask you. Saddlery! I mean, they're all mad.... They just drift around from one thing to another and they never get anything together ... (*Peter*, Fieldnotes, July 1982)

My own behaviour too, was not immune from such processes of critical appraisal.

> ... I think you've really set up this image, and they're ('The Clique') really frightened of you. I mean, I used to hear that you were analyzing us while you were in the pub. I mean ... didn't you used to go in 'The Roundhouse' once? ... I think they thought you were some kind of genius who segregates everyone into different columns and things. That's really funny because you're not that kind of person at all and they think you are ... (*Lennie*, Interview, December 1981)

In fact, it is possible to find multiple processes of personal authentication within the above quotation, since 'The Clique's' initial perception of me was itself deconstructed by Lennie who believed that she, and not they, had a more authentic understanding of my motives. This struggle for control over systems of meaning relating to the motives and personal identities of others, was central within students' social practice. Perhaps the most graphic illustration of its operation could be seen in Wendy's description of her friend Carol:

> ... I mean, I've never met anyone like Carol. She can justify anything. Any interpretation she puts her mind to. Like, she's justified sleeping around when she was in to that. She justified being celibate when she was in to that. She always argued against there being a thing called love, and now she's in love,

she justifies that. The thing is, you can't win. She's just so uncompromising about it ... (*Wendy*, Fieldnotes, April 1982)

However, the use of strategies of personal authentication like these created tensions for both female and male respondents. For males, these were evidenced in discrepancies between their behaviour in public settings and that which some female students observed more privately.

... But when I've been on my own with, those sort of people, they're completely different. When I'm on my own with Jim then he is really nice, quiet, sort of gentle person which he really is. But you wouldn't think that because of this image of being a tough leader ... (*Jane*, Interview, September 1981)

Whilst members of 'The Clique' seemed rarely to display their feelings or attitudes about cultural, intellectual and political matters in public, privately they were more willing to do so. Evidence for this was provided not only by comments made by female students but by my own fieldwork observations. When on their own, members of this group were quite capable of reflecting coherently not only on their own relationships with each other, but on political and cultural issues as well.

... I was reading this thing about Rosa Luxembourg the other day. She sounds a really amazing person — really strong. For her to have done all that is incredible. Sometimes I think I would like to get back into studying history and things like that ... (*Richard*, Interview, February 1981)

... I don't know. I've been thinking of moving to London, away from Spatown recently. But I don't know if I'd like it up there. There would be people that I knew, but not many of them, not unless a lot of us did it. ... But I think that I've got to get away and learn about new things and that ... maybe get back into college again ... (*Chris*, Fieldnotes, December 1981)

If there were differences between the social strategies male students used publically and those they used in more private settings, this was also true of females. While the latter remained relatively silent in public situations when males were present, they were more socially forthcoming privately and in single-sex groups.

Between late 1979 and early 1980, Wendy, Carol, Brenda, Jill,

Susan and Jane spent a great deal of time socializing with members of 'The Clique'. Fieldwork observations of their behaviour throughout this period showed it to be both restrained and quiescent. For the large part, activities tended to be dominated both verbally and physically by male members of the group. In contexts such as 'The Round-house', males frequently monopolized space by spreading their clothes over several adjacent seats and by throwing beer, peanuts, and crisp packets at each other. They also used strategies of conversational control, telling denigratory jokes about others present, talking and laughing at high volume and making comments of a sexist nature. Throughout this, females at first tended to remain relatively silent, smiling at males from time to time and stealing occasional glances at each other. When, later in the fieldwork, I questioned Susan about this behaviour, she commented.

> . . . The funny thing about all those girls who used to hang around with 'The Clique' is that none of them like each other. They just sit around and smile when they are out together. They never say anything. Like it was really funny the other night. I went down 'The Dugout' with Steve, Peter's brother, and there was Jill, Priscilla and Julie there. And there were so many women there who didn't speak to each other because it was so competitive. I mean, you don't want to say anything because you want to appear cool and sussed out and things like that. The chances are that if you say anything, someone will make a joke out of it. You can't be yourself in situations like that . . . (*Susan*, Fieldnotes, May 1982)

From these comments it would appear that males' efforts to verbally and physically dominate sub-cultural settings problematized considerably the kinds of interpersonal intimacy that students of both sexes were able to achieve. The public expression of personal motives and practices thereby becomes reserved for spheres of practice separate from those associated with much of sub-cultural activity.

It should be noted, however, that patriarchal control did not go unchallenged by female students. In mid-1980, for example, Wendy, Carol, Wanda and one or two others, began to meet regularly as an all-women group in public houses and clubs. Moreover, they began to engage in aggressive banter with members of 'The Clique', on one occasion pouring beer over them after overhearing sexist comments. In retrospect these occasions were regarded as personally significant by the female students involved.

... I think one of the best things about those days was going up to the 'The Roundhouse' in the evening. That was where we discovered feminism, politics, things like that, and started to fight back ... (*Wanda*, Interview, December 1981)

But the challenges female students gave to male definitions also had unintended consequences. It will be recalled, for example, that once they separated themselves physically from males in 'The Round-house', female students became labelled 'sweatshirt girls' and 'lesbians' by some of their male counterparts. Social stigmatizations like these, which work through the display of supposed intimacy with the sexual preferences of those to whom they are attributed, share a number of similarities with mechanisms of control prevalent in students' homes. Within these, we saw how the celebration of committed heterosexual competence and the identification and objectification of supposed homosexual desire, were strategies which culturally reproduced ideologies of monogamy and heterosexuality. Patriarchal surveillance and control within the home, operating through a double standard of expectations, therefore had its sub-cultural counterpart in male students' attempts to denigrate females via the sexuality attributed to them. Such continuities provide further evidence of the reproductive transportation of practices across sites of experience: in this case, from the home to that associated with sub-cultural activity.

For stigmatized social identities to be successfully attributed on others, insistent observation is required on the part of those who attempt the imposition. With this in mind, we can make better sense of the intensive forms of interpersonal surveillance to which respondents subjected each other. Social strategies such as sitting outside public houses, 'hanging around' in particular street contexts and spending time in large, open-plan settings, enable such interpersonal screening to take place all the more effectively.

Dress, Appearance and Cultural Acceptability

I argued earlier that cultural acceptability within students' homes came to be defined in terms of criteria connoting foreignness, exoticness and the everyday-once-transformed. These criteria also informed the style of dress which students adopted.

Males tended to wear clothes of three main types. First of all, there were those connoting early twentieth century 'affluence' and 'quality'. These tended to have been purchased from jumble sales and charity shops. During 1980, for example, white collarless shirts, cream jackets and pale cricket trousers were popular. By 1982, white collared shirts were being worn with bow ties, darker bagged trousers and braces. While such clothes connoted 'taste' through their past associations with 'leisured living', their modern-day recontexualization resulted in an overall style celebratory of affluence in economic recession.

> ... I was into a Somerset Maugham trip at the time, I supposed. Not colonialism, but the trappings of it, you know. Like crocodile-skin and canvas shoes, like pale jackets and cord trousers. I used to walk around in an old Harrods suit and straw trilby ...
> ... What did those clothes mean to you? (PA)
> ... They meant mod. Everything that I think mod means. ... When you're on the street, you're something special. You're not like everyone else. I don't know. I don't know. I was obsessed by olde worlde quality at the time ... (*Chris*, Interview, February 1981)

The second type of clothing worn by males was that purchased from army surplus stores — white T shirts, combat trousers, flying suits — urban guerilla chic. When asked about such clothing, respondents emphasized possibilities associated with the transformation of personal identity.

> ... I mean, the whole thing is, when you're pissing around, with not much to do and you've got these (combat trousers) on, then you can sort of imagine you're in another world ...
> ... How do you mean? (PA)
> ... Well ... sort of ... there's just you against them. You know, sort of like being in the PLO, something like that. You know, you have nothing else to you except yourself. You've just got the clothes you are in, nothing else. And they're clothes for doing things in! ...
> ... But they're British army surplus. Doesn't that mean anything? (PA)
> ... No they're not. They're Italian army surplus actually ...
> (*Jim*, Fieldnotes, March 1982)

Such descriptions suggest how the sedimented meanings of armed aggression associated with such clothing come to be transformed into those associated with challenges against an imaginary 'them', on the street, and even at the place of work:

... I mean, when I used to work at the burger place ... I just
used to spend all evening doing mindless things like cooking
burgers in a greasy steaming hole of a kitchen. And I would
look down from time to time at my trousers and boots just to
remind myself I was something else. I mean, like I used to
imagine I was on board some ship, like in wartime, cooking
this food. It was the only way you could keep going ... (*Phil*,
Interview, June 1981)

The final type of clothing popular with males was that which
conformed to criteria of foreignness. While both second-hand and
army surplus clothing required active work to transform their past
connotations, this third type of clothing operated with systems of
meaning which were more obvious in their impact. 'Fiorucci' shirts,
purchased on weekends in London, 'Benetton' trousers, purchased
locally, and 'World's End' African and aboriginal print shirts were all
occasionally worn as single items. Rarely, if ever, were they worn as
part of entire outfits in ways 'ready-made' by the stores selling them.

... No way would I do that. I mean, you'd end up looking
like some show-room dummy. I mean, you'd have to be really
thick, or something to do that ... (*Dave*, Fieldnotes, April
1982)

Towards the end of the fieldwork, 1950s American high school
and college clothes purchased from stores such in London proved
popular. These conformed simultaneously to all the criteria of cultural
acceptability so far described: being foreign, exotic, second-hand (and
therefore transformable) and demonstrable of quality by their connotations with American teenage affluence.

It was also possible to see similar principles of selection operating
with respect to respondents' choice of shoes. For the most part, these
tended to be classic in design — leather brogues, for example, were
popular with many males. Otherwise, foreign shoes such as Spanish-
made 'Kios', white cricket boot styled shoes, were popular. Towards
the end of the fieldwork, cuffed suede boots, purchasable only in
London, enjoyed some popularity. As soon as these became available
locally, however, and lost their connotations of exclusivity, they were
soon rejected.

Hairstyles also satisfied many of the criteria of cultural acceptability so far outlined. 'Foreign' styles were imported into Spatown from
London, Brighton, France and Italy when students returned from
visiting friends in these places.

... How come your hair's like that? (PA) (quiffed at the front,
shaved at the back)
... Well, everyone in London's got it like that now. I mean, I
just felt like some country idiot being up there. So when I got
back, I just had to have something done about it. Mind you, it
was really hard trying to explain what I wanted them to do
... (*Chris*, Fieldnotes, April 1982)

Other preferred styles showed evidence of a symbolic plundering
of those worn more locally as elements of mod, punk and skinhead
haircuts were combined together to create new overall effects. Relatively discrete sections of hair were vividly coloured, small sections
of the head were shaved, hair might be spiked or oiled, but rarely
were widely adopted styles copied in their entirety. Similar principles
also informed the self-presentation of female respondents. They too
bought many of their clothes from second-hand and charity shops,
choosing garments which connoted both quality and 'taste'. Cocktail
dresses and ball gowns proved popular early in the fieldwork. Preferred clothes which were more recently manufactured tended once again
to be foreign in their origin. 'Fiorucci' and 'Benetton' clothes were
frequently worn, as was French and American clothing. On some
occasions, however, the mode of self-presentation adopted by females
went further than this in that it sought to directly challenge middle
class ideologies of femininity. The wearing of torn T shirts, dirty
coloured sweatshirts and battered black unironed trousers can best be
seen in this light. Many of the items of clothing worn by female
students had been purchased from junk shops, charity stores and
second-hand clothes sales.

... Where do you buy your clothes now? (PA)
... Oh I don't know. Junk shops. It depends what I buy. I
mean, the majority of my clothes are jeans and jumpers, jolly
jumpers. I just buy whatever takes my fancy ... (*Brenda*,
Interview, January 1981)

... I think one of the best things to do is to go round jumble
sales on Saturdays. That's something that I really get a lot out
of. You can make some really amazing finds there. I mean, a
lot of the things that you buy are really good value. I bought
this really disgusting sixties' lurex top last week ... (*Barbara*,
Fieldnotes, October 1981)

Positive contrasts were often drawn between the clothes worn at the time of the fieldwork with those that had been worn some years previously.

> ... Yeah, If you could have seen us in those days, it used to be eyeliner, mascara, hair-spray, taking an hour to get ready before you went out, all that. And we used to wear these really uncomfortable shoes and hobble down the pub ... (*Wendy*, Fieldnotes, August 1981)

> ... I used to wear sort of skirts and very very dreadful platform shoes and tights and makeup. ... You know, 'Etam' clothes and lots of makeup ... You know, can you believe it, shopping at 'Etam'? It was terribly embarrassing really ... (*Lennie*, Interview, January 1981)

The reasons behind such denigration became clearer when I asked respondents for their opinions about those who currently wore 'High Street' clothes and make-up.

> ... You've only got to look at Sue and Katrina to tell that all they're after is being feminine and getting picked up by men. Those sort of secretarial-type women, with their pretty dresses and neat blouses and make-up they're all the same. They just pretend they're helpless in order to get attention. They buy their clothes from 'Top Shop' and 'Etam'. Urk ... (*Susan*, Fieldnotes, July 1982)

It makes sense therefore to identify as a motivating principle behind female students' hostility towards 'pretty' dresses, 'neat' blouses and make-up, their opposition to ideologies of 'respectable' middle class femininity. On the relatively few occasions when females wore dresses, these tended to be obviously elaborate and exotic. Jill's arrival by taxi at the social security office in a black cocktail dress and veil has already been mentioned, but other respondents too wore similar outfits from time to time. On such occasions, we should take care to identify the specificity of the targets challenged by such actions. As Jill's justification for her behaviour at the time makes clear, she did this, not in order to conform, to dominant ideologies of feminine practice, but in order to challenge her position of relative economic subordination at the time.

> ... Why did I do it? Well, I'm not having them sitting beind the desk thinking they're superior to me just because they have a lousy job sitting in the employment exchange ... (*Jill*, Fieldnotes, May 1982)

Opposition to class-based ideologies of femininity could also be seen in the way in which females dyed their hair. Many of them dyed it black, others streaked it with aubergine, orange or maroon.

> ... I remember that I was one of the first at college to dye my hair. I can still remember wandering into the refectory and everyone looking aghast and saying that it wasn't very feminine. They just would stare at me. It was shocking really. The colour, that it, all bright pink ... (*Brenda*, Fieldnotes, September 1981)

> ... I suppose I got into the 'Carmen' thing for a while. All black hair and heavy makeup, and dresses which I used to pick up in junk shops, things like that. It used to shock people but I didn't care. I think it was a really good image to be into at the time. A sort of forbidden image really ... (*Jill*, Fieldnotes, November 1981)

We can therefore see within both female and male students' style of self-presentation both the *affirmation* of cultural qualities originating within the home and attempts to *challenge* dominating modes of practice encountered sub-culturally.

Sexual Practice

Reference has already been made to the apparent contradiction between the open discussion of generalized sexual practice in students' homes and the absence of personal reference within this. I will now explore more fully some of the implications of this tension for students' own sexual experience. Every respondent in the study was heterosexually experienced at the time of the fieldwork and six of them had also participated in homosexual activity. Significant differences existed between female and males, however, with respect to the nature and commitment of the sexual relationships in which they had participated, and for this reason I will initially consider their experiences separately. Having done this, efforts will be made to explore the relationship between the sexual relationships entered into by respondents and those pursued by their parents.

Females

When the fieldwork ended, ten female students were involved in sexual relationships with members of the opposite sex. These varied in terms of their intensity and the length of their duration. At one extreme, was the relationship between Phil and Lennie which had lasted four years, regularly punctuated by breakdown following incidents of sexual infidelity on Phil's part. At the other, were relationships such as those of Norma and Barbara in which sexual involvement was organized on a more transitory basis with various members of The Clique'. Between these two extremes were relationships in which respondents had, for a number of months, cohabited with boyfriends. Wanda had lived away from home in a rented flat with her boyfriend for nine months by the time the fieldwork ended. Jane had lived at home with hers for about five months. Of respondents living at home, six regularly had boyfriends to stay over night. In each case, however, this was only allowed if parents had first been given the chance to screen the person concerned and to satisfy themselves that the proposed relationship was of some seriousness.

> ... One of the things which Mum always does if I ask a new boy back to the house is that she sits them down in the kitchen and asks them all about themselves, where they live, what they do, what school they went to, and so on. And then, afterwards, she either says, 'Oh, that was a nice boy', or she doesn't say anything, in which case you can tell that she really disapproves. She doesn't mind them staying overnight so long as she has seen them before ... (*Lennie*, Fieldnotes, April 1982)

Moreover, as the following comments make clear, permission for boyfriends to stay overnight was conditional upon daughters giving their parents advance warning of the prospective stay and committing themselves to relatively monogamous modes of practice.

> ... It would have been unthinkable for me to come home with a different boy every night. They would have thought that was too much ... (*Barbara*, Fieldnotes, December 1981)

> ... I couldn't have come home with a boy she (Mum) didn't know and spend the night together and then never see him again. She'd let it happen, but then she would get all funny about it ... (*Jill*, Interview, September 1981)

A few parents were rather more ambivalent in their reactions to boyfriends' overnight visits. Carol's mother, for example, felt it was important that her daughters should gain appropriate heterosexual experience, but showed a reluctance to allow Carol's own boyfriend to stay overnight.

> ... It's really important that at that age they should be exploring things about themselves. The problem is that it should be with the right person. I know that when the kids go off on holiday, they get up to all sorts of things, and it's good that they should experiment, and things like that, early on ... (*Mrs Smithson*, Fieldnotes, March 1981)

> ... There's something of a problem at the moment because Mum isn't happy about Steve staying overnight at home so I just tell them that I'm off to sleep with Steve, and they have to accept it. I mean, they know what we do, and if I can't do it at home, then they've got to accept that I will do it somewhere else ... (*Carol*, Fieldnotes, September 1981)

In situations like this students had little alternative other than to spend the night away in friends' flats and bedsits when sexual relationships were desired. Nevertheless, parents' efforts to encourage their daughters to pursue their heterosexual relationships with appropriate degrees of commitment seemed on the whole relatively sucessful. When I asked students whether they slept with different male partners on closely related occasions, their responses tended to be negative.

> ... No. I think it's important that you have a relationship with just one man at a time. I don't think you can give very much to a number of people at the same time. Besides, what they (the men) would say is that you weren't giving them much attention if you were having a relationship with more than one at the same time. I mean, there are some girls who sleep around, take the 'Nurses' (a group of nursing students who also went to 'The Roundhouse') for example, I mean, they just spent months trying to get off with each of 'The Clique' in turn, and they did in the end. But look at them ... (*Susan*, Fieldnotes, March 1982)

As Susan's comments make clear, female students' adherence to relatively monogamous patterns of heterosexual practice was not simply the result of processes of surveillance within the home, but was related also to the likelihood that they would be stigmatized by their contemporaries if they adopted alternative modes of practice. Personalizing serial monogamy was therefore the result of patriarchal control operating both inside and outside the home.

Homosexual relationships between female respondents were less frequent in their occurrence. Indeed, during the course of the fieldwork, they were referred to by only three respondents — Norma, Carol and a friend Patsie.

> ... Well, I think I wanted to see what it was like. I mean, I always felt that there was a part of me which hadn't been developed. I think it's nice for women to be that close and so it was really nice at the time. We'd all drunk a lot of wine that night and we'd been thinking about it for some time so it just seemed the natural thing to do. I've slept with Patsie a few times since ... (*Norma*, Fieldnotes, April 1982)

Interestingly enough, both Norma and Carol told their current heterosexual partners about the incident immediately afterwards.

> ... I mean, Carol went and told Stuart and apparently he said, 'Oh', and I told Ric and he didn't seem very interested, so that was that ... (*Norma*, Fieldnotes, April 1982)

When fieldwork ended, these relationships had discontinued, and their transitory nature and 'matter-of-fact' quality encouraged the feeling that they were valued perhaps more for their cultural acceptability as instances of exotic and not-yet-experienced practice, than deliberate attempts to challenges the limiting nature of either heterosexuality or monogamy.

It would therefore seem that the sexual practice of female students was organized in such a way as to do little to effectively challenge the limits that either heterosexuality or monogamy impose on social expression.

Males

The sexual practice of male respondents shared some similarities with that of females in that for the most part it was broadly heterosexual in nature. It differed, however, in that from time its serially monogamous nature was punctuated by brief periods in which parallel relationships of a less committed nature also took place. Indeed, a major source of tension between females and males was centred on whether primary sexual relationships were strengthened or weakened by concurrent less committed involvements. A number of males felt that this was true.

> ... I don't think it matters at all if you have relationships with other people, as long as you are sure about the other person. I mean, if you know that you mean a lot to them, then you're only going to let things go so far with someone else. I think problems stem from insecurity in the main relationship ... (*Doug*, Fieldnotes, March 1981)

Like Doug, most of them drew clear distinctions between personalizing and non-personalizing heterosexual relationships. But most were also aware of the dangers which less committed involvements posed for their primary relationships. Phil, for example, in talking about his relationship with Lennie, described the possible damage which Brenda could do if she revealed her knowledge of his other sexual partners.

> ... I suppose that one of the reasons why I don't trust Brenda is because of all the damage which she could do to the relationship between Wendy and me if she were to reveal some of the things which she knows about me and other people. All of those other people who, you know, don't mean anything to me ... (*Phil*, Fieldnotes, April 1982)

Further evidence of the operation of this strong classificatory relationship between personalizing and non-personalizing heterosexual relationships, was provided by male students' descriptions of the types of relationship they ultimately aspired to.

> ... I suppose that one of the things which might happen, well, which I reckon will happen really ... well, in the past I was really screwing around. And sometimes like, things would last for a while and we might have a good time. But in the main, it was really just like ending up in bed with someone at the end of the evening and not really caring about it. But I supposed that some day I will settle down and meet someone who I find everything in. Well, I suppose that I might ... (*Bill*, Interview, October 1981)

The contrast Bill draws between a past spent 'ending up in bed with someone' and a future in which he feels it will be possible to meet someone in whom he can find 'everything', suggests very clearly the operation of a principle identifying for him two qualitatively

different kinds of heterosexual relationship. Such a classificatory relationship did not underpin the practice of female students who emphasized the damage that usually occurred to primary relationships when
these were accompanied by parallel, less committed, heterosexual
liaisons.

Throughout the course of the fieldwork, only one reference to
homosexual activity between males was made, and this was within
the context of a drunken evening on holiday.

> ... We were on holiday, dossing around in Greece, and I can
> remember one evening when we were really pissed and we got
> back to the place where we were sleeping, and we felt really
> randy, so we rolled around a bit and tossed each other off. I
> mean, it was quite OK at the time. We've never done it since
> ... (*Doug*, Fieldnotes, January 1982)

In the light of this, it would seem that male students regarded
homosexual experience as personally less significant than did females.
For the majority of them, homosexual experience was infrequently
talked about and even more rarely experienced.

In the light of the evidence so far presented, it would appear that
the sexual practice of both female and male respondents ensured the
cultural reproduction of ideologies supportive of both heterosexuality
and monogamy. For females, such outcomes were achieved through
the effects of patriarchal surveillance both domestically and sub-
culturally, and as a result of the acquisition of particular subjectivities
which emphasized the importance of fidelity and commitment within
heterosexual relationships. For males, a strong classificatory relationship between personalizing and non-personalizing heterosexual
involvement had the short-term effect of encouraging a form of parallel sexual practice, but in the long-term contributed to the establishment of (at least temporary) heterosexual relationships organized
around notions of personal growth through industry and commitment.

It would be wrong, however, to underestimate the effect had by
parental intervention in securing these particular outcomes. Indeed,
parents' commitment to the attainment of these goals was witnessed
on numerous occasions when, in public settings, they recounted tales
which emphasized their daughters' and sons' heterosexual activity.

> ... You'll never guess what happened on Saturday. We had
> the plumber in doing some work on the hot water tank and I
> forgot to tell him that Martin and Patsie were in bed. Any-

way, he marched into Patsie's bedroom and caught them right in the middle of it. He was so shocked that I allowed such things to happen ... (*Mrs Jones*, Fieldnotes, March 1981)

Such public displays were in sharp contrast to the efforts parents made to normalize through counselling and therapeutic intervention suspected non-heterosexual behaviour.

... I don't know what to do about Tim at the moment. He worries me sometimes. He hasn't got any girl-friends, just that group of boys which he hangs around. I don't know if he's gay or something like that. I had a chat with him the other day about it and told him I'd arranged for him to go and talk with the marriage guidance people about it. Maybe that will help him ... (*Mrs Scotwell*, Fieldnotes, June 1981)

Paradoxically, while efforts like these were made to normalize suspected non-heterosexual behaviour amongst members of their own families, parents celebrated their acquaintance with openly gay men. The beginnings of an explanation for these apparent contradictions within household practice can, however, be identified in focal concerns operating pervasively within the cultural dynamics of students' homes. Interest in the culturally exotic, the foreign and the identifiably different positioned forms of sexual practice such as homosexuality firmly within the sphere of culturally acceptable experience. As a result of this, it should come as little surprise that gay men who were open and unambiguous about their sexual preferences were welcomed into the home. Militating against the unconditional acceptance of homosexual practice, however, were the threats it posed to the legitimacy of the nuclear family as a domestic unit, to particular divisions of labour between women and men, and to dominant ideologies about sexual pleasure and desire.

As Foucault (1979) has argued, processes of objectification and identification within discourses about sexuality are important mechanisms for the operation of power. We can therefore begin to see why it was that male homosexual practice could be acknowledged and validated within such settings only if it was *open, visible* and *unambiguous*, since by being thus it was more readily amenable to control through strategies of normalizing intervention. Homosexuality in an ambiguous or latent state posed a great threat to conventional gender relations.

Conclusions

In this chapter I have tried to explore the relationship between students' sub-cultural practice and that at other sites of experience. At a relatively superficial level we have seen how principles similar to those operating educationally and within the home informed sub-cultural practices as diverse as students' efforts to authenticate the social identities of their friends and acquaintances, re-define the meanings of public situations and locate types of paid employment which allow significant levels of personal freedom. Additionally, we have seen how the sub-cultural contexts preferred by students and the practices taking place within them were those which celebrated individuality and personal autonomy.

At a deeper level though it is possible to analyze students' home, educational and sub-cultural experience in terms of the power and control relations operating at each of these sites. Using the analytic framework suggested by Bernstein's (1982) research into the classification and framing of educational experience, it is possible to detect continuities across these three sites in terms of the strength with which experience was framed at each. By and large, these three contexts were weakly framed in that within each of them students were afforded considerable autonomy with respect to the negotiation of locational and interactional principles. Indeed, students showed antipathy towards those aspects of these experiential contexts where framing values were stronger.

There was also continuity within the classificatory relationships existing at each of these sites. The strong classification between *culturally acceptable* and *culturally non-acceptable* spheres of practice evident within the home, also operated as a central organizing principle influencing the way in which students negotiated educational and sub-cultural contexts. Similarly, the weak classification between work and leisure, established through parental practice within the home, informed both students' overall employment preferences and the manner in which they carried out the part-time work they undertook in local cafes and restaurants.

In the light of these insights, it would seem that the transportation of classifications and frames across sites of experience had important consequences for the cultural reproduction of key aspects of middle class habitus. The consequences of these transportations will be examined more fully in the next and final chapter of this book.

Chapter 6

Continuity, Transformation and the Reproduction of Class and Gender Relations

Introduction

In the last three chapters I have described the nature of students' experience at home, educationally and sub-culturally. In this chapter I will explore more fully the consequences of these practices for processes of cultural and social reproduction. I will begin by first identifying an appropriate framework for analysis. This will then be used to explore the broader social consequences of the student activities I have so far documented. In particular, attention will be focussed upon the role these play in processes of cultural and social reproduction.

Articulation, Celebration and Challenge

In chapter 1 of this book I argued that the major impetus behind this work came from recent ethnographic studies of young people's experience of schooling. In particular, my own fieldwork was influenced by those investigations which had attempted to identify the different ways in which young women and men from different class backgrounds negotiate their school and college experience.

Many of these studies have suggested that adequate forms of analysis require both an examination of the complexity of lived experience and a sensitivity to the possibility of developing modes of analysis which show the ways in which particular social practices can reproduce and transform existing social relations. Willis (1981) in particular has argued that the beginnings of such projects should be rooted in the ethnographic investigation of lived cultural forms.

> ... Though I will expand this more fully later ..., the point here is to suggest that for a properly dialectical notion of social

reproduction, our starting point should be in the cultural milieu, in material practices and productions ...

He suggests that researchers can best explore the way in which relationships between classes, genders, age groups and ethnicities are transformed and reproduced by first enquiring into the specificity of practices taking place at a distinctively *cultural* level. These active processes of cultural production which involve,

> ... the creative use of discourses, meanings, materials, practices and group processes to explore, understand and creatively occupy particular positions in sets of general material possibilities ...

constitute the lived experience of a particular group. By examining them in detail, and by investigating the nature of cultural production at different sites of experience, researchers can begin to identify the processes by which limiting forms of practice come to be culturally reproduced and by which the social relations that these give rise to come to be replaced.

In Willis's (1977) own investigation of the home, educational and sub-cultural life of a group of young working class men, he was concerned to identify,

> ... what is either absent or gestural in previous theories: resistance, lived cultural production of the working class: and culture as work in or on, formed by, and helping to form contradictions in the mode of production ...

As we have seen, a similar project came to be undertaken by Connell, Ashenden, Kessler and Dowsett (1982) in their study of Australian students' responses to schooling. Here too there was a concern to explore the relationship between home, school and sub-culture in making sense of responses witnessed at the second of these three sites. Moreover, their study too alerted us to the fact that households and families are not,

> ... closed universes, but places where larger structures meet and interact. We do not mean to suggest (here) that families are merely pawns in outside processes any more than schools are. In both cases, class and gender relations created dilemmas (some insoluble), provide resources (or deny them), and suggest solutions (some of which don't work), to which the family and the school must respond in its collective practice ...

In making sense of students' responses to schooling we must therefore be prepared to first explore the relationship between these and those at other sites of experience. Following this, it is important to examine the role that school and college-based responses play in reproducing and transforming broader social relations. But in order to do this effectively, we need first to identify in general terms the ways in which students can respond to school and college experience.

Until relatively recently, researchers addressing questions such as these have worked with somewhat crude conceptualizations of student responses to schooling, characterizing the latter far from consistently as, amongst other things, instances of 'accommodation' and 'adaptation' or 'resistance'. Before analyzing more closely the data collected during in this study, it would therefore seem sensible to spend some time developing a conceptually unambiguous framework within which to carry out the analysis.

Affirmation, Resistance and Contestation

From its recent origin in Hall and Jefferson's (1975) edited collection of essays *Resistance through Rituals*, through its refinement in the work of Willis (1977) and Apple (1982), we can trace a conceptualization of student 'resistance' as a countervailing tendency to the reproduction of existing social relations. Corrigan and Frith (1975), for example, were among the first to locate the concept of 'resistance' within the debate concerning the degree to which working class youth can retain some degree of autonomy in state institutions such as schools.

> ... Young people's experience is precisely the experience of the State's attempt ... to secure their contribution to the reproduction of capitalism. It is in this context that the notion of resistance becomes possible: the question is not whether working class kids can remain independent of bourgeois institutions (they can't), but what is the nature of their dependence, what are its effects on the work of particular institutions on the one hand, on the general processes of reproduction on the other ...

Willis's (1977) work extended these ideas to identify the role that schools play in shaping the form and nature of student 'resistance'.

> ... The institution of the school, for instance, determines the particular uneven patterns of extension and suppression of

common working class themes. This encourages an emphasis upon certain obvious forms of resistance specific to the school. In one sense, this is simply a question of inverting the given rules — hence the terrain of the school counter-culture smoking, proscribed dress, truancy, cheek in class, vandalism and theft ...

The conceptualization of 'resistance' which he offers is one which sees this as a symbolic act accomplished through working class culture, but which itself is directed largely against the material conditions which brought such culture into being. But Willis is also critical of analyses which look only at the transformatory potential of working class 'resistance'.

> ... For all its symbolic resistance, the moving spirit of working class culture to the present has been an accommodation to a pre-given reality, rather than an active attempt to change it ...

On many occasions, symbolically 'resistant' cultural practices act as accommodatory mechanisms, allowing those who express them relative autonomy within existing social relations while not threatening the existence of these in any way. By developing an analysis of 'resistance' which links it with 'accommodation', and in arguing as he subsequently does, that 'resistances' within school can ultimately contribute to the reproduction of existing class and gender relations, Willis highlights an important distinction between 'resistant' intentions and 'resistant' effects. 'Resistant' acts can therefore result in the reproduction of relations essential to the existing social order. As we saw earlier, MacDonald/Arnot's (1981a) work develops these ideas further to identify how more complex articulations between class and gender 'resistances' can also contribute to the social reproduction of class and gender relations.

Rather more positively, the radical and transformatory *potential* of 'resistance' has been taken up in Apple's (1982) analysis of the social consequences of modern-day American schooling. He argues that,

> ... Male and female students often expressly reject or contest the overt and covert messages of the institution. Reproduction and contestation go hand in hand. Therefore one cannot always assume that institutions are always successful in reproduction. No assemblage of ideological practices and meanings, and no sets of social and economic arrangements can be totally monolithic ...

Problems have arisen, however, when efforts are made either to associate the concept of 'resistance' with particular actions, or to specify the targets of individual acts of challenge. Anyon's (1983) work highlights many of these difficulties. In her account of the sub-cultural 'resistances' employed by teenage girls, for example, she talks of 'resistances' to dominant ideologies as well as to the following wide-ranging list of phenomena — stereotypes of femininity, stereotyped expectations, sexual attitudes, the alienation and degradation of everyday life, the female role, passivity, submissiveness, sexist values, present and future (sic) social discomfort, and contradictions imposed on girls in dress and behaviour. She further broadens her use of the concept to talk of both conscious and unconscious 'resistances', and links both of these to parallel processes of social 'accommodation' by which the meanings of dominating categories and practices are transformed by those who are dominated and oppressed. In a particularly unclear passage she claims that,

> ... Accommodation and resistance are integral methods by which females (and others) accommodate to what appears as if it cannot be changed, and appropriate, or resist, what appears to be changeable ...

While there remain considerable ambiguities in Anyon's account, her treatment of the concepts of 'accommodation' and 'resistance' is an interesting one, since it alerts us to the wide range of consequences that can follow apparently oppositional forms of practice. In recent years the concept of 'resistance' has come in for critical appraisal. Hargreaves (1982), for example, in questioning Anyon's use of the concept, which he takes to include,

> ... almost all pupil actions which do not count as absolute and willing compliance to teachers' demands ...

has argued that we need to develop a typology of modes of 'resistance' within educational settings which pays greater attention to,

> ... subtle and careful distinctions between different types of pupil activity ...

He cites with approval Woods' (1979) typology of modes of pupil adaptation to secondary schooling — a typology which like that of Merton (1957) from which it was derived — differentiates between the degree to which students accept the goals of schooling and the means by which it takes place. However, while this typology is an advance over less specific descriptions of student 'resistance', it has problems associated with it. Woods fails, for example, to develop an argument relating pupil adaptations within the school to the broader social relations which structure experience in educational and non-educational settings. Moreover, he fails to explain how particular modes of adaptation contribute to the reproduction and transformation of class, gender and age relations inside and outside schools. He further neglects to show how specific acts of challenge within one social context can selectively affirm modes of practice originating in other contexts with both continuous and discontinuous effects. In one sense, therefore, Hargreaves is correct in calling for a typology of modes of 'resistance'. In another, he falls short of the mark since the nature of cultural reproduction and transformation calls for more than a static pronouncement of *strategies of response*. Instead it calls for a generative *grammar of principles* which can account both for contemporary strategies of response and potential transformations of these. By developing this, it should be possible to account for both hegemonic and counter-hegemonic tendencies within closely allied sets of social practices.

In view of these as yet unresolved ambiguities, it is clear that a grammar of modes of 'accommodation' and 'resistance' should pay particular attention to the nature of that which is being 'resisted'. Moreover, if we are to retain a notion of cultural 'resistance' which simultaneously *affirms* sets of practices (perhaps from one site of experience) at the same time as it threatens others (at perhaps another site), we must specify the nature of that which is being 'resisted' (or affirmed) in a sufficiently *general* manner so as to enable the analysis of such articulations across sites. Now, Bernstein (1982) has argued that contexts can be distinguished in terms of their coding modalities; with *power* relations being reflected in classifications between categories and practices,

> ... We have argued that class relationships determine the principle of the distribution of power and the modalities of control. How? The principle of the distribution of power is made substantive in the principle of the classification which in turn creates the social division of labour and production ...

and principles of *control* being reflected in framing values within contexts,

> ... In the same way that the distribution of power regulates the classificatory principle via the social division of labour, so principles of control regulate framing via its social relations.

> ... Framing refers to the principle regulating the communicative practices of the social relations within the reproduction of discursive resources; that is, between transmitters and acquirers ...

In view of the generality of these claims, in the sense that any social setting can be characterized in terms of the modality of its coding, it should be possible to forge links between Bernstein's theory and conceptualizations of sub-cultural affirmation and 'resistance'.

In doing this, the first distinction we might usefully draw is between those symbolic challenges which are directed against fundamental *power* relations that act pervasively throughout society (and made visible; through challenges against classificatory relationships), and those which are directed against more localized principles of *control*. In developing this analysis further, it is necessary to bear in mind the possibility that actively 'resistant' subjectivities may or may not be accompanied by 'resistant' *behaviours*. Third, 'resistant' behaviours at one site of experience may on some occasions have as their focus, the way in which that context itself is structured. On others, however, they may be the result of 'resistant' intentions *displaced* or transported to that site. Fourth, we should take care to distinguish between actors' *intentions* and the *effects* that these may have. This last point becomes all the more important when we come to consider the role of articulations between practices across different sites of experience in the constitution of particular effects, since some of these practices may be affirmatory of, others 'resistant' towards, existing social relations. It is the *net effect* of these articulations between practices across different sites of experience which determines the extent to which effects are socially reproductive. We can, therefore, begin to talk about the effects of such articulations as establishing a particular *equilibrium between hegemonic and counter-hegemonic tendencies.*

With these points in mind, we can now begin to construct a generative grammar of modes of affirmation, acquiescence accommodation and 'resistance' within young people's educational and sub-cultural practice.

I have already drawn a distinction between those modes of challenge directed against relations of power structuring relationships between groups, and those directed against principles of control operating in particular settings. For the sake of conceptual clarity, I will call those challenges which are both subjectively and objectively directioned against power relations *intentioned resistances* (no inverted commas). These can be directed against power relations of various types:

against those constituting class oppression, gender oppression, ethnic oppression, age oppression and so on. Intentioned resistances, however, are likely to be occur relatively infrequently, since they presuppose that people have subjective insight into the objective nature of their oppression. Processes contributing to the establishment and maintenance of ideological hegemony are likely to militate against the development of such perspectives. Moreover, critical subjective insights and practices may, in themselves, be fleeting and transitory, occurring on only a few occasions at one or two sites of practice. It is only when subjective insight becomes *organized* in such a manner as to make links between the nature of oppression across sites, and in such a way as to recognize the shared nature of oppression, that we can talk of its systematic nature prefiguring radical practice. We may therefore distinguish between two 'moments' in the working up of intentioned resistance: one when critical subjective insights remain sporadic, isolated and unintegrated, and another when they become systematically organized so as to prefigure emancipatory practice (Giroux, 1983; Rothaus, 1984).

Systematically intentioned resistance can lead to several outcomes. First, it may contribute counter-hegemonically within power struggles. Praxis which seeks to free human agents from the limited possibilities allowed for by existing class, gender, age and ethnic relations does indeed, upon certain occasions and in certain contexts, work with emancipatory potential. On these occasions, systematic intentioned resistances have the potential to become *effective resistances*.

However, other less radical outcomes can flow from systematically intentioned forms of resistance. For example, efforts by new middle class youth to intentionally resist perceived class oppression within the school may, when constituted in the elaborated codes which characterize middle class linguistic performance (Bernstein, 1961) serve the opposite effect by reinforcing distinctions between different sets of class-based practices (Bourdieu, 1984). In such ways, systematic intentioned resistances can work contradictorily by contributing to hegemonic rather than counter-hegemonic tendencies. I will call this type of 'resistance', *reproductive resistance*.

Challenges against localized principles of control, on the other hand, are likely to take place more frequently since their existence does not presuppose that the social actors involved have insight into the nature of the power relations that structure localized interactional contexts. *Contestations* like these, which are directed against localized principles of control, may have as their object no more than the winning of degrees of personal autonomy within existing social relations. Furthermore, as I suggested earlier, some types of contestation may, in fact, be challenges *displaced* from contexts where control is felt more strongly.

Additionally, because the origin of localized principles of control may in some cases be the very power structures which are the focus of challenge in resistant modes of behaviour, contestations which have as their *intention* little more than the winning of individual and group autonomy, may as their *effect* challenge power relations within and beyond that particular setting. By so doing, they may on occasion become *effective resistances*. On the other hand, some types of contestation may further reinforce existing power relations, perhaps as a result of their having been constituted in modes of dominating practice. I will call these *reproductive contestations*.

Yet a further distinction can be made with respect to the consequences of challenges against power relations or principles of control. In particular, we can distinguish between challenges which have outcomes within the same set of power relations, and those which have outcomes within different sets of power relations. I shall call the consequences of this former type of challenge a *within-modality effect*, the latter an *across-modality effect*.

Finally, we need also to consider the existence of a variety of strategies of affirmation, acceptance and acquiescence. Strategies of affirmation include those practices which actively seek (both subjectively and objectively) to reinforce, support and affirm prevailing relations of power and principles of control. In the present study, such strategies were evidenced only infrequently in students' behaviour. In the case of acquiescence would fall those strategies which, whilst being subjectively challenging of power relationships and principles of control, are not accompanied by objective behaviours of either resistance or contestation. Some of these strategies are partially identified in the grammar of modes of challenge in table 4.

The usefulness of this grammar can be judged, at least in part, by its success in accounting for modes of response identified in recent ethnographic studies of young people and schooling. If, for example, we use this framework to analyze the data provided in Willis's (1977) account of male working class educational experience, it is possible to see how the 'lads' challenges, by and large, took the form of *contestations* directed against principles of control operating within the educational context.

A *Joey:* ... the way we're subject to their every whim like.
They want something doing and we have to do it, 'cos, er,

Table 4: A Partially Constituted Grammar of Modes of Challenge (Contestation and Resistance)

Target of acts of challenge	Power relations			Principles of control operative at the same experiential site			Principles of control operative at other experiential sites		
Subjectivity of agents concerned	Conscious challenge directed against power relations			Conscious challenge directed against principles of control at present site			Challenge directed against principles of control at other experiential sites displaced to present experiential site		
Objective behaviour of agents concerned	Individualized	Collective		None of challenge	Against principles of control at present site		None of challenge	Against principles of control at present site	
	INTENTIONED RESISTANCE	Counter-hegemonic	Hegemonic		Counter-hegemonic	Hegemonic		Counter-hegemonic	Hegemonic
		SYSTEMATIC INTENTIONED RESISTANCE		ACQUIESCENCE	CONTESTATION		DISGRUNTLE-MENT	CONTESTATION	
Effects (a) for the same set of power relations		WITHIN MODALITY EFFECTIVE RESISTANCE	WITHIN MODALITY REPRODUCTIVE RESISTANCE	MODES OF ACQUIESCENCE	WITHIN MODALITY EFFECTIVE RESISTANCE	WITHIN MODALITY REPRODUCTIVE CONTESTATION	MODES OF DISGRUNTLE-MENT	WITHIN MODALITY EFFECTIVE RESISTANCE	WITHIN MODALITY DISPLACED REPRODUCTIVE CONTESTATION
Effects (b) for other sets of power relations		ACROSS MODALITY EFFECTIVE RESISTANCE	ACROSS MODALITY REPRODUCTIVE RESISTANCE		ACROSS MODALITY EFFECTIVE RESISTANCE	ACROSS MODALITY REPRODUCTIVE CONTESTATION		ACROSS MODALITY EFFECTIVE RESISTANCE	ACROSS MODALITY DISPLACED REPRODUCTIVE CONTESTATION

Note: Such a grammar takes as its starting point the existence of subjective challenges on the part of agents. It should be possible to construct a similar grammar of affirmations and boredoms, which would take as its starting point the absence of such subjectivities. It is probably best to conceive of hegemonic and counter-hegemonic tendencies as dialectically related to one another. Reproductive resistances contain at least the seeds of effective ones.

Source: Aggleton, P.J. and Whitty, G.J. (1985) 'Rebels without a cause?: 'Socialization and sub-cultural style among the children of the new middle classes', *Sociology of Education*, 58, January, pp. 60–72. Reproduced with permission from the American Sociological Association.

er, we're just, we're under them like. We were with a woman teacher in here, and 'cos we all wear rings and one or two of them bangles, like he's got one on, and out of the blue, like, for no special reason, she says, 'Take all that off'.

PW: Really?

Joey: Yeah, we says, 'One won't come off's'. She says 'Take yours off as well'. I said, 'You'll have to chop my finger off first'.

PW: Why did she want you take your rings off?

Joey: Just a sort of show like. Teachers do this, like all of a sudden they'll make you do your tie up and things like this. You're subject to their every whim like ...

B Joey: The chief occupation when we'm in the hall is playing with the little clips that hold the chairs together. You take them off and you clip someone's coat to his chair and just wait until he gets up and you never really listen ...

Interestingly enough, this is *not* the conclusion which Willis himself reaches. Instead of seeing these actions as straightforward challenges directed against *principles of control* within the school, he argues instead that they are oppositions to *mental labour* in general.

> ... It is the school which has built up a certain resistance to mental work and an inclination to manual work.... In a strange unspecified way, mental labour henceforth carries with it the threat of a demand for obedience and conformism. *Resistance to mental work becomes resistance to authority as learned within the school* ... (*Willis*, 1977, emphasis added)

Of course Willis's own interpretation of these actions could possibly be supported by unpublished ethnographic data. Unfortunately, never in the published transcripts of his interviews do we find evidence suggesting that the 'lads' challenges were clearly and unambiguously, intentionally and practically, directed against mental labour *per se*, still less against power relations which establish and legitimate the distinction between this and other kinds of work. This would seem all the more unusual in view of Willis's (1981, 1982 and 1983) own insistence that the ethnographic investigation of lived experience should be the starting point for the generation of theory. I would therefore argue that the data which the reader is presented with in *Learning to Labour* is more consistent with the view that the 'lads' challenges were directed against control within the educational setting rather than against broader power structures. As such, these actions should best be viewed as *contestations*, not resistances.

At the level of effect, however, these modes of contestation have an important role to play in consolidating classifications between mental and manual labour (through their selective affirmation of elements of manualism), and between female and male spheres of practices (through their constitution in patriarchal discourses about masculinity and manliness). The former of these effects is thus an instance of *within-modality reproductive contestation*. The latter is an example of *across-modality reproductive contestation*.

Similarly, the so-called 'uncouth language and behaviour' used by some of the young women in Connell, Ashenden, Kessler and Dowsett's (1982) study of ruling class schools is best viewed as an attempt to challenge principles of control within them. In this case, however, what are essentially *contestatory intentions and behaviours* have resistant effects, since the appropriation and display of 'non-feminine' modes of conduct effectively challenge the broader power relations structuring female and male spheres of practice. In this study we therefore find evidence of a different kind of effect to that described by Willis. The young women described by Connell *et al*, in contrast to the young men described by Willis, *effectively resist across modality* the relations of power which ensure the existence of differentially evaluated modes of gendered behaviour. These practices, therefore, have a role to play in counter-hegemonic moments within processes of cultural and social reproduction.

There is also an example of *intentionally resistant* actions contributing to 'unintended' and hegemonic tendencies in McRobbie's (1978) description of the social practices of the group of working class young women she studied. Her work graphically illustrates how her respondents were able to use working class ideologies of femininity to simultaneously *contest* principles of control within the classroom and *intentionally resist* the power relations which privilege more middle class modes of feminine conduct. Ultimately, however, the actions of her respondents have culturally reproductive effects, since they consolidate the classification between female and male spheres of practice. Because of this, McRobbie's study provides evidence of both *across-modality reproductive contestation* (challenges againt pedagogic processes) and *within-modality reproductive resistance* (challenges against particular ideologies of femininity) contributing to common effects. Thus, social practices which both contest and intentionally resist class-based gender representations can contribute, through processes of

reproductive contestation and reproductive resistance, to the reproduction of existing class and gender relations.

At this point it is useful to use the grammar outlined earlier to
make sense of the social practices of students in the present study.
Throughout my own fieldwork, I too noted instances of challenge
directed against aspects of gendered practice. Sub-culturally, female
respondents' verbal and physical assaults on males were associated
with a concern to win ideological 'space' from patriarchal surveillance
and derogation. These behaviours, which are not only sub-cultural
challenges in their own right, may also be *displaced* challenges working
against similar processes of patriarchal control operating within the
home. There were however limits to effectiveness of challenges such
as these, since although females would sometimes separate themselves
from males in this way, on subsequent occasions they adopted more
acquiescent social practices in their dealings with men. Similarly,
while male students put on make-up, dyed their hair and wore relatively unconventional clothing, their motivation to do this was
driven more by a desire for success in competition with other males
for females, than by a wish to radically challenge existing gender
relations.

I would therefore argue that these challenges were *contestations*
directed against principles of control operating in the settings in which
they were displayed and towards the winning of relative autonomy
for students to choose the contexts and occasions on which to display
certain femininities and masculinities. They are neither intentioned
nor effective resistances since they do little to challenge the fundamental, patriarchally constituted, power relations that ensure the
differential evaluation of female and male, heterosexual and homosexual spheres of practice. Still less do they challenge the power
relations that maintain distinctions between personalizing and non-
personalizing forms of sexual practice. Instead, they work seeking
ideological 'space' within the discourse of the categories created by
dominant classifications. Additionally, the success of such challenges
in winning limited degrees of personal autonomy was very much
dependent upon their being constituted in middle class modes of
elaborated verbal communication. Because of this, they act simultaneously as *across-modality reproductive contestations*, contributing to the
cultural reproduction of linguistic strategies which serve as material
markers of class differences.

Throughout the fieldwork, it was also possible to observe challenges directed not so much against modes of gendered practice as
against the pedagogic dimensions of social contexts. Many of these

were witnessed in interactional contexts which I have already characterized as strongly framed. For example, every student interviewed
had attempted, whilst at school, to verbally challenge the authority of
teachers as well as other aspects of the schooling process which were
not amenable to personal control. This contestation of the *positionality*
inherent in certain types of schooling and the welcoming of those
contexts which allowed the 'release of the person' were important
features within students' educational practice. Moreover, challenges
like these were, at least in part, linked to the simultaneous affirmation
of personalizing modes of practice encouraged within the home.
However, once again the fact that such contestations were themselves
constituted in forms of elaborated interpersonal communication does
much to reinforce a specific class-based cultural arbitrariness around
differences in verbal expression. The use of modes of interpersonal
communication which celebrate personal control over systems of
meaning thereby becomes a key strategy within which respondents
come to reproduce forms of habitus intimately connected with their
class location. I would therefore argue that *within modality reproductive
contestations* such as these also contribute to hegemonic moments within the cultural reproduction of limiting forms of class practice.

However, students also sought relative autonomy of expression
within existing class relations. A dissatisfaction with the personalizing
possibilities perceived in academic study encouraged many of them to
undertake forms of paid employment outside Spatown College.
Moreover, popular forms of employment were those which offered
negotiable working conditions, the chance to meet 'interesting people'
and a weakening of the distinction between work and leisure. Routinized work in offices and factories, characterized by respondents as
'shitty jobs' were systematically rejected. Thus, whilst formally wage
labour, preferred modes of employment were those perceived as pro-
viding additional opportunities for the extension and development and
'release' of the person. They were forms of work which offered
students intellectual and personalizing possibilities as well as enhanced
personal income at a stage in life when many of their contemporaries
were themselves in relatively disadvantaged circumstances.

Yet another illustration of students' efforts to win ideological
'space' within existing class relations can be seen in the challenges
which they directed against those 'received' modes of dress and
appearance associated with 'High Street' shops. Such challenges, working in part by an affirmation of elements of cultural exoticism, encouraged respondents to explore both *upwards* and *downwards* options
via their own style of self-presentation. The wearing by males of

Appendices

Appendix 1: Students' home backgrounds

Students	Household	Household status	Parents' occupations
Dave	Lane	Single parent (f)	Adult educationalist and FE lecturer
Nigel and Wendy	Stewart	Single parent (f)	University lecturer and Community artist
Peter	Richmond	Two-parent	Civil servant and Primary teacher
Ric	Cooper	Two-parent	Joint owners of educational toy shop
Chris and Jackie	Williams	Single parent (f)	Art college teacher and No paid employment
Tim and Elaine	Scotwell	Single parent (f)	Actor and FE lecturer
Stuart and Patsie	Jones	Two-parent	Primary teacher and HE lecturer
Jill and Robin	Francis	Single parent (f)	Guest house owner and Art teacher
Barbara	Blare	Single parent (m)	Community artist and No paid employment
Tom	Wiley	Two-parent	University lecturer and Painter
Carol	Smithson	Two-parent	Community carpenter and Potter
Brian	Simpson	Two-parent	Civil servant and No paid employment
Brenda	Miller	Two-parent	University lecturer and Welfare officer
Norma	Green	Single parent (f)	Secondary teacher and Designer
Jane	Burton	Single parent (f)	Playgroup organizer and Antiques dealer
Susan	Turner	Single parent (f)	Architect and No paid employment
Lennie	Deutsch	Two-parent	University teacher and Primary teacher
Wanda and Pam	Wilson	Two-parent	Nightclub proprietor and FE lecturer
Phil	Lines	Single parent (f)	Shop worker and HE lecturer
Jim and Bill	Grant	Single parent (f)	Primary teacher and Actress

Appendix 2: Students' educational backgrounds

At the time of their registration at Spatown College, students posses-sed a minumum of 5 GCE Ordinary level passes at grade C or above.

MACDONALD/ARNOT, M. (1981b) 'Theories of class and gender reproduction and the case of girls' education', paper presented to the Political Economy of Gender Relations in Education Conference, Ontario: Institute for Studies in Education, October.

MARCUSE, H. (1969) *An Essay on Liberation*, Harmondsworth: Penguin Books.

MARX, K. (1932) *Die Deutsche Ideologie*, published as MARX K. and ENGELS F. (1965) *The German Ideology*, London: Lawrence and Wishart.

McCALL, C.J. and SIMMONS, J.L. (1969) *Issues in Participant Observation*, Reading, MA: Addison Wesley.

McROBBIE, A. (1978) 'Working class girls and the culture of femininity', in Women's Studies Group, *Women Take Issue*, London: Hutchinson.

McROBBIE, A. (1980) 'Settling accounts with sub-cultures', *Screen Education*, 34, pp 37–50.

McROBBIE, A. and GARBER, J. (1975) 'Girls and sub-cultures: An exploration', in HALL, S. and JEFFERSON, T. (Eds) *Resistance Through Rituals*, London: Hutchinson.

MERTON, R.K. (1957) *Social Theory and Social Structure*, Chicago: Free Press.

MOORE, D. (1972) 'Why teenagers do "A" levels at the tech', *Times Higher Educational Supplement*, 21 April.

POLLARD, A. (1985) *The Social World of the Primary School*, London: Holt.

POULANTZAS, N. (1975) *Classes in Contemporary Capitalism*, London: New Left Books.

RAPOPORT, R. and RAPOPORT, R. (1976) *Dual Career Families*, 2nd edn, London: Martin Robertson.

RATTIGAN, B. (1978) 'A study of students opting for further education at 16', unpublished PhD thesis: University of Manchester.

ROSZAK, T. (1968) *The Making of a Counter-Culture*, London: Faber and Faber.

ROTHAUS, L. (1984) Personal communication.

ROWE, D. and SLATER, P. (1976) 'Studies of the psychiatrist's insight into the patient's inner world', in SLATER, P. (Ed.) *Explorations in Intrapersonal Space*, Volume 1, London: Wiley.

RYLE, A. and LIPSHITZ, S. (1974) 'Towards an informed countertransference: The possible contribution of repertory grid techniques', *British Journal of Medical Psychology*, 47, pp. 219–25.

RYLE, A. and LUNGHI, M.E. (1968) 'The measurement of relevant changes after psychotherapy: Use of repertory grid testing', *British Journal of Psychiatry*, 115, pp. 1297–304.

SCHATZMAN, L. and STRAUSS, A.L. (1973) *Field Research*, New Jersey: Prentice Hall.

SCHOOLS COUNCIL (1970) *Sixth Form Survey. Volume 2A Full-time Courses in Colleges of Further Education*, London: Schools Council.

SIMMON, G. and TROUT, G. (1967) 'Hippies in college: From teeny boppers to drug freaks', *Transaction*, 5, pp. 27–32.

SLATER, P. (1972) 'The measurement of consistency in repertory grids', *British Journal of Psychiatry*, 121, pp. 45–51.

SMITH, H.W. (1975) *Strategies of Social Research*, New Jersey: Prentice Hall.

TAYLOR, I., WALTON, P. and YOUNG, J. (1973) *The New Criminology*, London: Routledge and Kegan Paul.

TAYLOR, I., WALTON, P. and YOUNG, J. (1975) *Critical Criminology*, London: Routledge and Kegan Paul.

THOMPSON, E.P. (1963) *The Making of the English Working Class*, London: Gollancz.

TRUSTRAM, S.F. (1967) 'School or college? A consumer's viewpoint', *Vocational Aspect of Education*, 19.

TURNER, G. (1983) *The Social World of the Comprehensive School*, London: Croom Helm.

WERTHMAN, C. (1963) 'Delinquents in school: A test for the legitimacy of authority', *Berkeley Journal of Sociology*, 83, pp. 39–60.

WEXLER, P. (1983) *Critical Social Psychology*, London: Routledge and Kegan Paul.

WHITTY, G. (1985) *Sociology and School Knowledge*, London: Methuen.

WIEDER, D. and ZIMMERMAN, D. (1974) 'Generational experience and the development of freak culture', *Journal of Social Issues*, 30, 2, pp. 137–61.

WILLIAMS, R. (1958) *Culture and Society*, London: Chatto and Windus.

WILLIS, P. (1977) *Learning to Labour*, Farnborough: Saxon House.

WILLIS, P. (1978) *Profane Culture*, London: Routledge and Kegan Paul.

WILLIS, P. (1981) 'Cultural production is different from cultural reproduction is different from social reproduction is different from reproduction', *Interchange*, 12, pp. 48–67.

WILLIS, P. (1982) 'Male school counter-cultures', in Open University, *Popular Culture*. (U203) Block 7. Unit 30. Milton Keynes: Open University Press.

WILLIS, P. (1983) 'Cultural production and theories of reproduction', in BARTON, L. and WALKER, S. (Eds), *Race, Class and Education*, London: Croom Helm.

WILLIS, P. (1984) *Youth Unemployment: Thinking the Unthinkable*, mimeo, Wolverhampton Youth Service

WOLFENSTEIN, M. (1951) 'Fun morality', in MEAD, M. and WOLFENSTEIN, M. (Eds) *Childhood in Contemporary Cultures*, Chicago: Chicago University Press.

WOMEN'S STUDIES GROUP (1978) *Women Take Issue*, London: Hutchinson.

WOODS, P. (1979) *The Divided School*, London: Routledge and Kegan Paul.

WRIGHT, E.O. (1978) *Class, Crisis and the State*, London: New Left Books.

WRIGHT, E.O. (1980) 'Varieties of Marxist conceptions of class structure', *Politics and Society*, 9, pp. 323–64.

YOUNG, M.E. (1971) 'A survey into the social and educational background, aims and achievements of full-time "A" level students at Burnley Municipal College, 1969–70', DAS (TE) dissertation, Bolton College of Education.

Name Index

Subject Index